THE ART OF
QUALITY DEBT
COLLECTIONS

EXPLORING THE HUMAN SIDE OF COLLECTION

DARRYL D'SOUZA

authorHOUSE®

AuthorHouse™
1663 Liberty Drive
Bloomington, IN 47403
www.authorhouse.com
Phone: 1 (800) 839-8640

Published by AuthorHouse 08/20/2019

ISBN: 978-1-7283-2392-3 (sc)
ISBN: 978-1-7283-2390-9 (hc)
ISBN: 978-1-7283-2391-6 (e)

Library of Congress Control Number: 2019912259

Print information available on the last page.

This book is printed on acid-free paper.

This book is dedicated to those of you who enjoy credit risk management. I hope this book helps you carry out your work with a new perspective and allows you to stir the hearts and minds of the many people you work with in your field. I would love nothing more than to see this book in the hands of all the members of your teams and have them move in the direction I've laid out.

It's a great challenge and a mindset change. Take your time, do it right, and enjoy.

CONTENTS

INTRODUCTION

Financial institutions have gone through a series of developments in recent years, from a time when most activities in banks, credit institutions, cooperative societies, agricultural and trade associations, and the like were conducted manually to the point where modern IT systems and infrastructure are broadly adopted and applied to every facet of these institutions' day-to-day activities. Despite the current speed and quality of services rendered, only one section of financial and credit institutions' operations remains the same and unimproved. This is the collections department.

The collections process used by many financial institutions and agencies has languished in a substandard state for far too long. It is a boring, energy-sapping, and cantankerous activity for most collections officers and their clients. What is wrong with this approach? Why haven't financial institutions figured this out after so long?

Thanks to my decades of experience as a banker and seasoned trainer of financial institution personnel, I realize that what is missing in the practice of collections is any apparent interest in genuine customer service. Until this moment, the relationship between a typical collections officer and a client who borrowed money but has defaulted in repayment has been like that between a cat and a mouse. There is a constant feeling of acrimony and misunderstanding.

Without a doubt, what is causing all this uneasy feeling between collections officers and clients is that banks and other financial institutions fail to see the duty of a collections officer the way retail companies see the duty of a cashier at a register collecting money from shoppers. In retail settings, customer service is unparalleled. There are warm greetings, thoughtful body language, friendly facial expressions, and other genuine attitudes that make shoppers eager to keep making their purchases from the same company or store. Why can't the process of collections be done in the same way?

This book is written to introduce a new and fresh idea of the way collections should be done all over the world. It is my sincere expectation that this book will be quite useful for everyone in the collections department as well as those who conduct similar exercises as part of their regular profession or a part-time activity.

ACKNOWLEDGEMENTS

In my almost three decades of working at various multinational banks—including ANZ Grindlays Bank, HSBC, Standard Chartered Bank, Citibank, J.P. Morgan Chase Bank, First Gulf Bank, and the Royal Bank of Scotland—I have come across several individuals who have largely contributed to the development of my skills in banking as well as in other areas of personal achievement.

I am grateful to Mr. Tony Morgan for his invaluable advice on the issue of collections when I was working at Standard Chartered Bank. The bulk of my experience in the management of credit facilities has come from the workshops and conferences I attended at Standard Chartered Bank and Citibank. I also gained significant practical knowledge in this field from most of the banks I worked in throughout my career.

I appreciate the efforts of my mentors in the banking industry—Mr. Ray Galliott, Mr. Tony Morgan, and Mr. Fadel Al Ali—for their selfless and conscientious assistance that grounded me in the area of credit and collections, from which I derive the confidence to call myself an expert in this field. This is not an idle boast: several years of my professional experiences in the banking industry were absolutely dedicated to credits and collections.

There are so many other people I would like to thank here, but there is no space to do so. All I can say is that I am indeed grateful for your contributions, big or small, to my career development as an experienced credit and collections professional.

I would also like to thank my colleague Mrs. Carmen Louis. I have worked with her for the last six years, and she inspired me to write this book. Her dedication and expertise in collections and her strong conviction that quality in collections can yield stellar results has been a testament to me in penning this book.

A PERSONAL STORY

I began my banking career almost thirty years ago at the ANZ Grindlays Bank in India, where I was a credit card collections and operations officer. It was in this position that I started viewing collections as a vital aspect of the banking industry. In addition to helping banks and other financial institutions increase their revenues and proactively tackle bad loans, collections can be an avenue for gaining loyal and happy clients. How do financial institutions make clients happy even when those clients are slow to balance up repayments? Good and heartfelt customer service is the key.

Unfortunately, this is what is lacking in banks and financial institutions. When it comes to recouping non-performing loans or unpaid credits, the relationship between collections officers and clients can turn feisty and uncomfortable. This is where it is fair to say that something is quite wrong with the current collections practices out there.

In the early days of my banking career, financial institutions would often collect past-due loans and credit card bills through reminder letters and phone calls. Those approaches were rigid and lacked empathy. I am fully aware that collections officers are not supposed to be babysitters, but they need to feel what their clients are feeling—they need to, even for the briefest moment, put themselves in the position of their clients. This is the essence of practical and effective customer service.

During the early 2000s, my eyes were opened to some preventable shortcomings that constantly kept the collections arm of the financial institution on the path of underperformance. Most collections departments have poor training in place for their officers. It is regrettable to say that most of the elements of training offered by some financial institutions lack the active ingredients required to transform the attitudes, performance, and track record of their collections officers.

In everything that involves dealing with a customer, it is essential that efforts be made to reach out in a respectful and mutually cooperative manner. But that is not what goes on in the collections departments of most banks or financial institutions. Instead, collections officers, over several calls and client visitations, turn into some kind of bully that customers or clients do not want to have anything to do with.

Experiences in the late 2000s and early 2010s opened my eyes, and I noticed that the common approach was riddled with what I personally refer to as *attention deficiency collections system*. Even when collections officers do everything in their power to be good at calling default clients or customers, they still do not understand that this process is more about listening to their clients than talking. Their attention span is limited, and this causes major misunderstanding between collections officers and their clients. In the course of listening to customers, collections officers should be able to feel what their clients are feeling and offer the best solutions to get loans, credit, and other financial responsibilities settled with little or no hassle or headache.

I set out to write this book to offer my decades-long credit risk and collection experiences for people in the field to digest. Some of the information in this book was actually taken from the series of in-house training and consultancy services I have offered to many financial institutions all over the world. It is my humble gift to those who are concerned about managing credit facilities and collections processes. I hope that this book will accomplish its primary aim and help financial institutions simplify the process of debt collection by emphasizing the human side.

We should never assume that creditors and debtors are enemies or two sides of a coin. They should instead be partners in progress and resolve the issue that has brought them together as amicably as possible.

CHAPTER 1

Ten Attributes of Great Customer Service

The term *customer service* only rings a bell for people when it's referring to the retail industry. Everyone understands that for store or shop owners to keep people coming to their businesses, they must demonstrate a great deal of genuine and practical customer service. This may range from smiling when offering to help shoppers pack their things to showing deep and heartfelt respect whenever customers are around. Can you imagine entering a restaurant or bar where the attendants are rude and unsympathetic? Would you ever go there again? Would you recommend that restaurant to your friends and colleagues?

Today, banks are losing customers in droves, in thousands, every year. According to a report in *Forbes*, a Bain & Company-supported survey of 137,034 customers in twenty-one countries revealed a gloomy picture for financial institutions: about 29 per cent of customers globally said they would switch banks the following year if they could easily do so. That is nearly a third of banks' current customers. This is not a healthy trend for financial institutions. One of the ways for a bank to maintain the same number of customers, according to the report, is to improve its salesmanship.

Salesmanship could mean selling a bank's best products and solutions to current and prospective customers. But how can a bank's collections officers approach existing customers who have defaulted on loan repayments without offending them? How can collections officers broach this delicate subject without driving customers to defect or approach another bank for services? This question is the inspiration for my concept of introducing practical customer service techniques into collections procedures.

Both financial institutions and their clients stand to gain a lot when the collections process leaves neither party bitter, angry, or vengeful. This kind of great salesmanship—or dedicated customer service, as we will describe it—won't happen overnight. Financial institutions need to consistently train collections officers in this new and practical approach to recovering debts. Below are ten attributes of effective and great customer service.

1. Having the Patience to Listen and Think

Great customer-service professionals are patient, listen to clients or customers, and spend an appreciable amount of time thinking and reflecting on what they have heard. Most of the time, collections officers think they are entitled to a superior position in a discussion with a client who has defaulted on repayment. Collections officers with unimpressive track records do not see their clients as a people like them, worthy of respect, consideration, and kindness. The main issue here is that no one communicates when everyone is talking at the same time. Not only do good listeners grasp the issue on the ground from an omnipresent angle; they also have the unique opportunity to contribute meaningfully to the matter, having fully understood the conditions that led their clients to act the way they did.

Unfortunately, we live in a loud and misguided society that rewards bullies and considers a quiet and reserved personality a sign of weakness. Yet the type of collections officer who brays at top of his lungs or bangs on tables to express anger and frustration with a slow-paying client will achieve nothing significant. This is the wrong way to do customer service. Behaving in such a deplorable way is comparable to an impetuous teacher who tries to instill knowledge into erring students by shouting hoarsely at them. Instead of communicating anything, that teacher is instead instilling fear into the students' minds and making them uncomfortable with learning both inside and outside the classroom.

2. Inspiring Courage

When clients who have defaulted on a repayment approach you, you can be sure that they are ashamed and scared. These clients may find it very difficult to communicate in a meaningful way. As a collections officer who fully understands the power of great customer service, you have a duty to cheer these people up and make them speak up. You will never achieve any tangible outcome meeting with a client who is not in good mood because of a failure to settle financial obligations as promised. And if you come to the meeting breathing fire and brimstone, you will surely end up pushing such clients back into their inactive shells.

When nothing reasonable and coherent is discussed during a meeting, the possibility of getting a client to provide a workable repayment plan is remote. Have you ever seen how salesclerks at shopping malls help very old and young shoppers accomplish their purpose? That is exactly the way we should approach talking with or holding a meeting with clients whose self-confidence has already been damaged by their failure to fulfil the promise of a timely debt repayment or settlement. The next time you are standing or sitting in front of such a discouraged person, try to stay calm, collected, and welcoming. To make a success of your collections efforts, create an atmosphere of true friendship and not one accusing or bullying.

3. Knowing the Customer Is King

Is the customer always king? The answer to that question is very simple: yes, the customer is always king. It doesn't matter how long your client has fallen behind in repayment or how much an individual currently owes your institution. You should accord each client the respect due to a customer you and your bank are not interested in losing.

Of course, that is not the current reality in collections practices. Some people think they have to be harsh, rude, and coercive to compel a defaulter to pay up. This wrong notion is sold to many collections officers, even by their own employers, be they banks, credit associations, or cooperative societies. When defaulting clients hear about a collector calling or visiting, they are driven into a state of powerlessness if they don't immediately have the means to pay off their loans and other owed credits.

Instead, think about the way a king is treated in a community. Being in that position does not immediately turn a king into a god, but it inspires honor, respect, and obeisance. You are not required to worship your clients who owe your institution some amount of money, but be respectful and courteous in your dealings with them. Respect begets respect. If you want someone to take you seriously and listen to your complaints, you must first be willing to show some measure of respect.

4. Using Positive Body Language

Your body language in debt collections must be positive, firm, and meaningful. What comes out of your mouth must be compatible with the way you walk, your facial appearance, and the way you move the rest of your body. Remember that you are in front of someone—a defaulting client—who is carefully monitoring and watching every step you take. You don't want to appear fake or unable to genuinely communicate the feeling you have in mind toward the concerned client.

It doesn't matter where you are working or who you are attending to, in terms of demographics, culture, norms, or values. What really matters is the sincerity of your feeling toward a particular client. It pays to learn or have pre-knowledge of your client's cultural and personal values so that you won't cause some chaotic circumstances by being unknowingly disrespectful. This is why your body language must be positive and consistent with your honest intention and plan to help your client get over loans, credits, and so on.

Collections officers who cross the line and act impudently toward their clients will not only escalate problems but won't be able to make any tangible progress toward their primary responsibility. Are you aware that collections duty is like fighting a war? If you are going to win, you must be sure of your weapons and the way you are going to deploy them. One of your weapons of client disarmament and active engagement is positive body language.

5. Being an Understanding Person

In successful customer-service operations, it is important to know what or who you are dealing with. How can you know your client inside and out if you are not an understanding person? Being understanding means you are patient, caring, and helpful enough to identify the pain spots in your client's life. And you are doing everything you can to bring some relief while simultaneously carrying out your designated functions.

In order to be an understanding person, you must be willing to exhibit a high degree of flexibility. This means being ready to set aside your own priorities and think about what will help your clients solve their immediate financial problems. Think of this like someone on a missionary assignment; in spite of your own sins, you are doing all you can to convert another sinner.

To be honest, this involves letting down your guard and personal arrogance and, to a certain degree, seeing the world through the eyes of your clients. It may not be easy at first, but if you persistently practice this virtuous attitude, you will surely master the art of knowing what causes a problem for your client and how it can be proactively resolved.

6. Being a Problem-Solver

It is not enough to be kind, considerate, and understanding; you must also be willing to bring all your human virtues together to help someone who is in need of dire financial help to resolve his problems. On most occasions, collections officers do not necessarily perceive themselves as problem-solvers. Some even complicate problems on the ground with their uncouth attitudes or utterances. This does not mean that you have to be an alpha and omega to all your clients, but there are instances when, due to your professional experience, you know exactly what your clients could do to overcome their financial problems. Instead of being quiet and uncooperative, speak up and offer some time-tested solutions that can bring everything under control.

Here is the catch: the earlier your clients are able to offset their debts, the better for you and the institution you are representing or working for.

It is like the relationship between two hands: one washes the other. That is how great customer service works. It is a mutually beneficial relationship.

7. Saying "I'm Sorry"

Don't get infuriated just yet. We are talking about effective customer service, and this entails doing the impossible. One of the things you will never hear from some collections officers is "I'm sorry" when they go overboard in the course of carrying out their functions. Some cases that could have been amicably resolved end up in court because the collections officers broke civil laws while exerting their authority to recoup the loans that have remained non-performing for a long time.

You can learn to simply apologize if you discover that your previous actions have compromised ethics and offended your client. In this way, you are deliberately creating a comfortable atmosphere for negotiation. It is just common sense that no one wants to engage in chitchat with someone who has embarrassed or abused them. It takes a little courage to say "I'm sorry" and right the wrong that you had done to your client.

8. Going the Extra Mile

The most effective customer service arises from an awareness that doing your best may not be enough at times. It is the habit of going the extra mile that counts and makes things revolutionary. Once again, salesclerks at the shopping mall can give us a clear example. After you dump your selections on the counter, a salesclerk immediately springs into a series of actions. She will help you pack the things in a bag, process the payment, give you your change if you have any, and in some cases assist you in putting the bag in the shopping cart. Within a few seconds or a minute, she has done three or four great acts of service for her customer.

As a collections officer, there are plenty of things you can accomplish within a few minutes for your clients. How about going through some financial records with them? How about helping them calculate their finances in order to identify any opportunity for paying off their debts? How about acting like an Agony Aunt, assuring them that everything will be all right? In a matter of two or three minutes, you may succeed in calming troubled souls and positioning them to be ready for financial responsibility. One great attribute of efficient customer-service officers is that they know it is not doing the assigned duty that matters, it is adding value to what was done that is memorable to the client.

9. Accepting Feedback

No one can be an island to oneself. The same ideology is applicable in the world of customer service. As a collections officer, you need constant feedback from your clients as well as your colleagues and supervisors/managers to be very good at what you do. What are your clients saying behind your back? If you are the type who kicks up dust everywhere and treats your clients with utmost disrespect, you will surely create a bad aura.

This negative perspective of your professional disposition may affect your career as your institution recognizes that you aren't a well-rounded collections officer. You will not be put in the bracket of top performers, and this may affect every other aspect of your activities as a professional. This doesn't mean that you should play to be liked by clients and fail to do your primary duty; it just suggests you should be conscious of your delivery style, making sure that it satisfies ethics and the degree of professionalism laid down by your employer. Most importantly, you should not pursue an agenda that will compromise the sanctity of your profession. Financial services professionals are expected to be cautious and deliberate and follow some standards while carrying out their statutory responsibilities.

10. Making a Difference

The difference you are called to make in the life of your client surpasses merely helping him organize his finances so as to be able to repay his final obligations. It includes creating value in the course of doing your job. Making the collections task a better one for everyone begins with seeing your job as a unique opportunity to contribute your little quotas to making the world a better place.

When you help people overcome their most difficult problems, you are making our world a better place. You are making a strategic difference. As in the retail industry, customer service should make life easier for the clients/customers involved; it should help them alleviate some pain spots in their lives. It should not be an exercise that adds to people's worries and concerns. Rather, it should create a long-lasting impression in the minds of clients and happiness in the heart of the customer-service provider.

Note that there is no one-size-fits-all in customer service. From one location to another, the customer-service process is purely influenced by local customs and traditions. While in some countries bowing is a way of showing respect and honor, in others such demonstrations of respect may not be necessary. It is imperative to understand that cultures and personal manners play a significant role in the delivery of high-class customer service.

References

Du Toit, G., and Burns, M. "Many Banks Are Losing Customers and Don't Even Know It." *Forbes* (December 15, 2016). Retrieved from https://www.forbes.com/sites/baininsights/2016/12/15/many-banks-are-losing-customers-and-dont-even-know-it/#35933c1d2935.

Friedmann, S. A. "The 10 Commandments of Great Customer Service." *The Balance Small Business* (November 25, 2017). Retrieved from https://www.thebalancesmb.com/ten-commandments-of-great-customer-service-2295997.

CHAPTER 2

Risk-and-Reward Relationship

The financial industry has gone through series of dramatic changes since individual or personal banking was first introduced in 1975. It has transitioned from manual operations to high-speed computerized banking system through the adoption of management information systems (MIS).

Consumer Credit as a Financial Product

Consumer credit has been a vital product in the financial industry for centuries. Individuals as well as businesses borrow money in the form of loans, lines of credit, mortgages, credit cards, motor vehicle finance, store cards, retail loans (retail installment loans), and so on. The consumer credit department is one of the biggest arms of every bank or financial institution, and it has expanded, both in scope and variety, over the years. Even though credit initiation, scoring, and approval procedures have been systematically improving, the collections process still needs some fine-tuning or improvement to be compatible with the requirements/demands of the twenty-first century.

Credit Initiation, Scoring, and Approval Processes

For consumers seeking to secure credit in the form of loans or mortgages, for example, the procedures have changed from the way they used to be. It is still imperative, however, that consumers go through well-arranged

9

procedures, starting with an application form that requests all the necessary personal information the financial institution requires to process the loan. Next, consumers will be subjected to a series of screenings that include but are not limited to the following:

- **Judgmental screening**—Credit officers use their own discretion to judge an application for credit.
- **Scoring**—Credit scores are used to determine if customers are qualified for the loan they have applied for.
- **Credit-bureau screening**—Some external credit-screening bureaus can be contacted to conduct extensive screening to discover if the customer is creditworthy.
- **Debt-burden screening**—Credit officers check to see if past debts may prevent the customer from accessing newer financial credits.
- **Customer verification**—Personal information the customer makes available to the financial institution is verified for accuracy.
- **Collateral verification**—Credit officers ensure that posted collateral is commensurate with the amount of credit the customer has applied for.

Financial institutions are currently using two approval systems—preapproved and post-screening. With the post-screening method, customers will get a loan or line of credit approved after successful completion of all essential screening. A preapproved system, on the other hand, gives customers instant access to the credit or loans they have applied for before the financial institution conducts any screening on the customer or the application. Other factors, such as a high credit score and great financial transaction history, may help customers secure preapproved credit facilities.

The Collections Process

Banks can seem very friendly and supportive when a customer regularly keeps the promise of repayment. However, the tune automatically changes when the same customer defaults on repayment terms on several occasions. The once robust and friendly relationship between the bank and its indebted customer immediately sours. The bank, through its appointed collections officer, initiates a series of actions against the customer that may, unfortunately, undermine its usual customer service. There are six steps in the collections process used by financial institutions around the globe.

1. Initial Contact

A credit officer appointed to recover a bad loan will first make contact with the defaulting customer. In today's modern banking, this could be through a signed letter, email, telephone call, telegram, or other traceable means of contact or communication. At this initial stage, the officer simply briefs customers about their failure to pay up their loan and hints that the bank is concerned about it. Elaborate discussions and negotiations are not expected at this level.

2. Service

The bank organizes a little customer service show by approaching the defaulting customer with the aim of learning exactly what was responsible for the inability to pay up. This may be done through a series of phone calls and letters. The wording or content of the letters will have a soft tone, and the phone calls may appear friendly and sympathetic. This initial air of empathy is intended to let customers know that their bank is willing to listen to them and understand why it has been difficult to make their repayments. Unfortunately, this empathy won't last long, as banks, represented by their collections officers, will soon strike an entirely different tone that may seem more like coercion.

3. Locate

If collections officer cannot reach a defaulter directly and express the institution's grave concern about the matter, tracing the whereabouts of the defaulter is often the next step. This may require the officer to travel from one location to another to find out where the defaulter is in person. A collections officer will go through the information provided on the initial application to discover where the defaulter lives. Banks sometimes utilize the service of an external agency to help them find the current address of the defaulter.

4. Collections

This refers to the actual collection of the debt and is only possible if the defaulter's location has been identified or has not changed from the previous one recorded in the form or other documents with the bank. Sometimes a customer has moved from the address or location given to the bank. In that situation, it will be difficult to get in touch with the customer. The collections officer has to move on to the next step, which is skip-tracing the customer.

5. Skip-tracing

This involves tracking the defaulter to another physical address or location in case the previous address is no longer valid or correct. This may happen if new employment, marriage, and other life events cause customers to change their address but they are slow in informing the bank. Customers may move from one city to another, but it shouldn't be a hassle for banks to discover this if the customer is a registered resident of the new location.

6. Selling

If the customer cannot repay the loan or other credit product owed to the bank, the collections officer may suggest selling the debt. Debt-selling has been in practice for several years, and it has even become a big business in the financial world. Nowadays, countries and companies issue debts that are sold in the public to investors. They do this to raise money that will be used in running the day-to-day affairs of their businesses. In a similar approach, an individual defaulter may choose to sell debts to another debt-receiving company. And if the lender—a bank or other financial institution in this situation—agrees with the terms, defaulters can be relieved of their debts through this process.

Some of the negotiating tools collections officers can use in helping customers solve their debt problems include the following:

- **Rewrites**—The terms of lending and borrowing may be rewritten. Some banks may agree to new terms of lending when they realize that defaulting customers have no apparent means of paying off their debts.
- **Extensions**—The number of years scheduled for repayments may be extended. The point of rewriting loan terms is to give defaulting customers more time to repay their debts.
- **Partial payments and settlements**—The collections officer and the defaulting customer may agree to a partial payment by which a certain fraction of the total amount owed is repaid or settled.

In the absence of mutually agreed-upon solutions from negotiations, the defaulting customer has an option of going for personal bankruptcy. This route will be governed by the bankruptcy laws in the country where the customer resides. The lender (bank or another financial institution) may also decide to use external and secondary agencies to help it recover the money. Or it may opt for legal recourse by turning the case over to attorneys who will work toward using a court action to compel the defaulter to pay up.

As simple as they appear, collections procedures can sometimes be cumbersome and poorly carried out, and they may end up having unanticipated outcomes. The defaulting customer's feelings may be hurt in the process by the rudeness and inconsiderate attitude of the collections officer. Something has to be done to input genuine customer service into collections procedures.

Managing a Collections Department

The way each financial institution manages its collections department has far-reaching effects on the professional attitudes of their collections officers. If anything has to change in the approaches adopted by collections officers, the collections department of every financial institution must take strategic steps to answer some challenging questions.

What Is the Capacity of the Collections Department?

The capacity planning for a collections department will reveal its ability to undertake the collections responsibilities imposed on it by the financial institution. Some collections departments are too small and poorly equipped for the tasks placed on them by their parent institutions. This could affect the quality of the services rendered by collections officers.

What Are the Contact Techniques?

Typical contact techniques are telephone calls, mail (letters), email, and home visits. Are the collections officers trained on how to do these contacting procedures while remaining passionately concerned about helping clients or customers solve debt problems? This is the essence of bringing human feeling to their jobs. They need to perceive the defaulting customers as partners in progress rather than enemies whose feelings don't matter.

How Does Duty Decentralization Improve the Collections Process?

In the banking industry, collections officers are the most overworked group of financial service professionals. To make life easier for them so that they will not transfer their frustration to defaulting customers, their duties must be decentralized. This entails dividing their periods of engagement or operation into days and hours—in other words, a collections officer should not be on the road collecting debts every day, Monday to Friday. Collection work should be scattered over some hours or days per week, but not every single day.

Failure to decentralize these duties can leave collection officers overwhelmed by such an enormous task. They will then transfer their aggression to their defaulting customers. The customer, in turn, will immediately recognize a lack of heartfelt customer service in the attitude of these officers.

How Can a Collections Department Be Most Successfully Managed?

The goal of every financial institution is to set up and maintain an effective collections department that can get the job done. This involves the following four distinct processes:

1. **Hiring**—This first strategic step must be carefully undertaken to find the right candidate for the position of collections officer. It is important that banks get their hiring procedure right from the beginning. They should look for professionals who demonstrate the confidence and compassion required for impactful customer service. The qualities of empathy and kindness are in their character, not in their academic qualifications. Financial institutions go amiss by concentrating on paper qualifications and not the personality traits of their new hires.

2. **Training**—The training given to new recruits should emphasize both ethical considerations and the need to carry out their assigned duties compassionately and without an iota of prejudice. This is the attitude that is needed if institutions want to achieve the same level of heartfelt customer service as is found in the retail industry. Collections officers need to know that defaulters are human beings who may actually be helpless and hopeless due to circumstances beyond their control. Collections officers should be trained to be patient and empathetic; they should put themselves in the position of their defaulting customers and feel the pain of whatever is going on in their lives. This is what genuine customer service entails.

3. **Compensation**—Collections officers should be well paid for jobs that demand a lot of physical and emotional dedication. It is wrong for financial institutions to attach remuneration or commission to the performance of collections officers. This will put pressure on the officers to make as much commission as they can. They may inadvertently set aside ethics and empathy to compel defaulting customers to pay up. This is where the genuine customer service that banks earnestly desire disappears. Collections officers should never be seen as a debt-collection machines but as human beings

dealing with other people's problems and helping them overcome financial challenges.

4. **Supervision**—It is not enough to tell newly hired collections officers the right and ethical things to do on the job; banks must also supervise their professional dispositions. This will give the institutions a chance to quickly correct an erring collections officer who acts unprofessionally or unethically.

It is not news that some financial institutions are feeling the pinch from their collections officers' inappropriate behaviors toward defaulting customers. Some have lost customers at an unprecedented rate. Some banks are struggling to get people to apply for their credit facilities. This may be due to negative reports about unethical debt-collection methods.

To resolve this sensitive issue, banks may adopt automated collection systems in which human errors and prejudices do not exist. Defaulting customers receive automated messages every now and then to remind them to settle their debts as scheduled. In this situation, the defaulters are unlikely to be offended. If an automated debt-collection machine can do such a great job of collecting debts, why can't human collections officers?

Risk-Management Techniques

All financial institutions with a collections department aspire to operate it in a way that drastically reduces the institution's level of risk exposure. The primary aim of running a personal or consumer credit facility is for the financial institution to profit from the operation. In the face of mounting risks, banks may forfeit expected rewards and deal with losses annually. This is why the issue of risk management at the collections department is a very sensitive topic.

How can effective risk management be instituted in a bank's collections department? The following are the essential steps that must be taken by financial institutions to achieve risk-free operations:

- **Routine credit/line management**—Efforts must be made to manage the credit already provided to customers. This may require some routine checking of customers' accounts to notice their performance. Good loans are used for active purposes, such as manufacturing and trading. Bad loans, on the other hand, are non-performing, and customers with these non-performing loans may not be able to repay them on time.

- **Hierarchy**—It is helpful to establish a hierarchy or stages of authority in the collections department. A senior credit/collections officer may be in charge of managing or overseeing the actions of junior collections officers so as to make sure they conform with the professional ethics their position demands. Risk-prevention procedures should be managed by officers divided along the hierarchy, empowered by their rank to inspect, correct, and inform junior colleagues in the department how to mitigate risks in the course of doing their jobs.

- **Credit-policy committee**—This committee is expected to meet regularly and fashion processes or procedures for controlling risks in the collections department. The committee can also set up an audit division that will oversee both system and personnel auditing. It is possible to identify operational lapses during the auditing and call the attention of the credit-policy committee to it. In order to rectify the errors, the committee may choose to make new rules and regulations that will help collections officers make risk-free decisions during their operations.

- **Consistent training**—It is a fact that collection officers can never have too much training. Their job is so delicate they sometimes have to make snap decisions that are reasonable and practical. A bad decision can put their financial institution at risk of losing customers and money. Even though there are strict rules of engagement, dealing with unpredictable human beings can lead to unimagined outcomes. Training should be a continuous exercise to transform collections officers into functional specialists.

Increasing Rewards

Every financial institution that incorporates personal and consumer credit in its operations does so to make money. But because this is a very risky financial venture, the best approach for increasing profitability is to consider the following actions:

- **Loss reduction**—Financial institutions should devise a system for recognizing losses early and taking appropriate action, such as writing off bad loans, repossession, or foreclosure. With these, lenders can quickly cut their losses while searching for profitability in other transactions they are involved in.

- **MIS**—Management information systems help banks to easily identify problematic portfolios using leading, coincident, or lagging indicators. MIS also helps in financial documentation and data retrieval, making it possible for banks to properly document all their financial transactions.

- **Specialized financial products**—Banks can provide products that are capable of increasing profitability rates, including indirect lending and shelter finance. The good thing about these specialized products is that they have well-designed techniques for appraisal, management, and collections. For example, business-vehicle dealers allow some individuals to buy cars through loans directly from dealerships. The loans are indirectly provided by the banks via the dealerships. The car dealers undertake the appraisal of the customer's loan application and monitor the loan repayment pattern. If the customer defaults, the dealership will arrange for the repossession of the car. Banks do not need to send collections officers after the car buyer and can save money through this approach.

References

David B. Lawrence. *Risk and Reward (1984).*

CHAPTER 3

Debt Collectors Shouldn't Be Bullies

The first chapter of this book dealt with best practices in customer service. The second highlighted the risks and rewards associated with banks and other financial institutions running credit facilities or departments as a vital part of their financial operations or transactions. These two chapters provided the necessary foundation for the themes expanded on in the remaining chapters of this book.

At first glance, it is hard to imagine collections officers acting as bullies while dealing with defaulting customers. However, recent happenings in the financial industry indicate that some collections officers abuse their clients' rights in this way. In the United States, a law was enacted to address this unprofessional act. The Fair Debt Collection Practices Act of 1978 provides guidelines that collections officers or agencies must follow so as not to undermine the fundamental human rights of their defaulting customers. The law suggests civil liability against any debt collector who breaks the provisions in the law. In principle, collections officers are discouraged from using such unethical approaches for collecting debts as the following:

- harassment or abuse of the defaulting customers
- false or misleading representations
- unfair practices
- rude and improper communication practices

The Fair Debt Collection Practices Act (FDCPA) primarily focuses on protecting the defaulters' right to humane and lenient treatment while negotiating terms of repayment. The ethics and legal provisions guiding the actions of collections officers will be described in detail in Chapter 9.

In the meantime, outlined below are some of the acts of bullying that have been identified by some concerned defaulting customers.

Harassment

Some defaulters have complained of being harassed by unprofessional collections officers. The harassment can happen in a variety of forms, the most common of which are verbal and physical harassment. Some defaulting customers have been approached menacingly by collections officers who acted like they were going to punch the defaulters in the face for not paying up. Others have complained of being verbally abused, derided, and threatened by some uncouth collections officers.

To fully understand what constitutes harassment, here are some acts that can be regarded or adjudged as harassment in various societies:

- grabbing people by the arm or shoulder to get their attention or force them to speak with you
- raising a middle finger in an attempt to be disrespectful
- holding a woman's hand to get her attention
- using words that can be considered racially charged or sexist
- knocking on doors of defaulters at the wrong hours of the day— too early or too late at night
- sending letters to defaulters' houses regularly
- hiring people to oppress or catcall defaulters on the street or at their places of work or residence
- sending accusing voicemails or text messages
- trying to block defaulting customers from driving out of their driveway

Nuisance Calls

Another unprofessional way some collections officers inconvenience their defaulting customers to is to place numerous nuisance calls. They do this at odd hours of the day. A defaulter may be awakened by a phone call from a collections officer. Sometimes, the call comes later in the day or just before bedtime. These calls indicate that a collections officer has paid little or no attention to the communication training received. A defaulting customer who is being hounded here and there by annoying phone calls will find it difficult to sit down with the same impudent officer to negotiate how to repay the debts.

If you, as a collections officer, don't know what would be considered a nuisance call, you should be sure to avoid the following:

- **Calling at strange hours of the day**, like two or four in the morning; even eleven or twelve at night is an inconvenient time to call anyone for anything
- **Making annoying two- to three-second calls** as many as twenty or forty times a day—an absolute no-no when dealing with defaulters.
- **Using public phones to call defaulters** when they have stopped answering your calls when you used your office number or your personal cell phone number.
- **Hiring call centres to help you disturb your defaulters** with horrendous calls until they respond with something reasonable.
- **Requesting that your defaulting customers provide you with private information** that may include their family members' phone numbers or their employers'.

Physical Threats or Use of Violence

Some defaulters have had to deal with physical threats from unscrupulous collections officers or their representatives. These may include a show of physical force or a threat of it. It is wrong for collections officers or their representatives to physically molest defaulting customers. That singular action can amount to breaking the law, and it basically violates the ethics laid down by most banks for collecting due or past debts.

The idea of sending a collections officer to a defaulter is to use all available resources at the officer's disposal to persuade the defaulter to pay up. Such resources do not include threats or a show of force. Think about it this way: It will be difficult to persuade a defaulting customer who has been physically molested by a collections officer or the officer's representative to continue to use the bank's services. News spreads quickly, and it may not take long for other customers to become aware of the shoddy treatment and turn away from that bank as well.

Inappropriate ways that some collections officers have physically and violently abused their defaulting customers include the following:

- punching customers in the face or on any other part of the body
- hitting defaulting customers' cars with their own
- throwing objects at defaulters during meetings or negotiations and calling them displeasing names
- banging on tables when the negotiations don't proceed as they expected, thinking they need to show their annoyance
- Looking menacingly at defaulting customers
- using threatening statements like "I will deal with you!" or "I'm going to show you hell!"

Obscene and Abusive Language

It is improper for collections officers to use obscene and abusive language against defaulting customers to coerce them to pay their debts. Collections officers must pay serious attention to their choice of words to avoid hurting customers' feelings. It is going to take some apologies for a customer whose feelings have been hurt to overlook the matter. This is why collections officers are trained to be very cautious in the use of words. They need to be selective in the words they use to address their customers, defaulting or not.

From one society to another, there are some words, expressions, or language choices that are deemed to be obscene and abusive. A professional collections officer should refrain from using any of the following:

- words that refer to male or female genitalia or any other parts of human body that suggest sexism or sexuality
- words that are considered to be racial or ethnic slurs
- words that are disrespectful of people's religious beliefs
- words that denigrate people's cultures, including their food, fashion, way of speaking, and table manners
- words that undermine people's status in society

Public Shaming

It is a bad approach to publish the names of defaulters with the intention of forcing them to pay their debts. It could breach customers' privacy rights. Releasing unauthorized personal information about people could have a far-reaching impact on the reputation of the financial institution involved in the process. This could lead to a huge lawsuit that may negatively affect the financial status of the bank or financial institution whose collections officers acted inappropriately.

The following public-shaming procedures have been found to cause serious problems or troubles for the collections officers who did them, together with financial institutions they represented:

- posting damning information about defaulters on social media or the internet, whether collections officers do it themselves or pay someone to do it
- paying for a full-page advertisement in a magazine or newspaper to shame a famous person who owes your financial institution
- pasting handbills or posters close to the residence of the defaulter because you think it will have a destructive impact on that individual
- paying gangs or thugs to spread fake information about the defaulter
- hiring publicists to put out information that can destroy the reputation of the defaulter

- using any available medium, online or offline, to shame defaulting customers

Collection of Unauthorized Fees or Charges

A collections officer cannot ask the defaulting customer to pay for phone calls, transportation to and from the customer's residence, or any unauthorized fees that were not included in the initial agreement between the financial institution and the customer. Doing that will amount to committing a crime or engaging in a scam, which is punishable by law. Collections officers should do their job respectfully and methodically. They should utilize the nuggets of wisdom delivered to them during their training to interact with their customers.

As a professional collections officer, do not carry out any of the following unauthorized and criminal activities:

- asking your defaulting customer to pay for your transportation to and from the place of negotiation, promising to be soft during the negotiations in return.
- asking to be paid for the time spent during the negotiations. You are not a waitress/waiter at a restaurant requesting a tips; you are a professional who is paid for the job you are doing.
- charging defaulting customers for services done under your normal duties as a collections officer. Your monthly salary is meant to compensate you for your efforts at helping your customers pay up. Don't add to their financial burdens.
- charging for communication expenses. Don't ask defaulting customers to pay for your phone bills or other expenses incurred while doing your statutory functions as a collections officer.
- expecting your defaulting customers to reimburse other expenses you have incurred while trying to get in touch with them

Acquisition of Location Information

Bank customers are expected to provide their legitimate or correct locations when applying for loans or credit facilities. However, in the course of time, they may move from one location to another but fail to inform the bank or its officers. When this occurs, as a professional collections officer, you should follow only the legal and ethical avenues available to you to obtain their new addresses. In some circumstances, difficult customers may want to hide their new address. Never let emotion or anger get the best of you and break laws by doing the following:

- **Searching around for the defaulters in order to get their new location information**—Some collections officers have resorted to following defaulting customers from their workplace to shopping centres and other public places. Such an action can be considered to be stalking, which is against the laws of any country.
- **Contracting private investigators to follow defaulters around**—You are breaking laws when you encroach upon people's human rights. We all have the liberty to protect our privacy. When you hire private investigators to go after your defaulters, you are infiltrating their private lives.
- **Illegally accessing personal information from public records**—These include utility companies, local government offices, schools, courts, and law-enforcement agencies. It may be illegal to collect sensitive personal information without receiving prior permission to do so. It is advisable to act within the confines of the law.

Unprofessional Communication

Without being repetitive, it is important to emphasize that your communication as a professional collections officer should be moderate, sensible, and effective when negotiating or engaging in any form of verbal or nonverbal interactions with defaulting customers. Highlighted below are four attributes of great communication in debt management:

1. **Selflessness**—Don't just concentrate on keeping up your side of the argument. Listen to your defaulting customers so that you can make informed decisions during negotiations.

2. **Middle-ground philosophy**—Do all you can to find a middle ground in debt communication. Never aspire to be the only one talking while your customers listen passively. Leave room for mutual understanding by actively involving defaulting customers in conversations or negotiations.

3. **Mannerisms**—Your mannerisms during communication are important. If you are rash and inconsiderate, defaulting customers will be intimidated. This may spell doom for the negotiation. Be patient and realize that you need customers' cooperation to achieve any tangible results in the debt collections process. If that is lost at the beginning of your communication, you may not be able to get it back through the negotiation process.

4. **Clear and concise language**—Don't use business jargon or parlance that may confuse customers. They really need to catch every point you discuss during the negotiations so they can respond properly to all your requests.

False or Misleading Representation

It may be rare, but it sometimes happens that unprofessional and rabble-rousing collections officers engage in false or misleading representations. They do not strictly follow the rules given by the financial institutions they are representing. A false or misleading representation to defaulting customers can come up in various ways. As a collections officer, you are not doing your job properly if you do the following:

- **Attempt to change prior agreements or terms without the knowledge of your defaulting customer**—You may even intimidate your customer, but the information you are relaying to them is untrue and your own fabrications

- **Ask for concessions on issues that your financial institution has not mandated you to make**—For example, don't ask your defaulting customer to bear part of the expenses incurred before and during negotiations. Your bank should have made arrangements for those expenses

- **Ask defaulting customers to change previously recorded personal and financial information without a standing directive from the bank you are representing**—Only your bank has the power to make such sensitive changes and it must be done with the full understanding of your customer.

- **Present false arguments in lieu of genuine negotiations**—You must take every word you utter seriously, because a lie can hurt your career when the truth surfaces in the future. The financial institution you represent has a lot to lose when its reputation is sullied by your false and misleading representations.

- **Sugar-coat your communication with the intent of defrauding your defaulting customers**—Remember that your customers are in a very dire situation and will hold on to any promises you made during meetings or negotiations.

Unfair Practices

Collections departments (or collections officers) at many financial institutions engage in unfair practices. In principle, the FDCPA was established to provide much-needed protections for bank customers who will or have secured loans and other financial credits that must be repaid at a certain point in time. The act recognizes the following attitudes or activities as unfair practices against defaulting customers:

- abusing them verbally and physically
- demonstrating violent attitudes that can have a psychological or emotional impact
- presenting false or misleading information

- using unauthorized and illegal approaches to obtain pertinent or sensitive information
- asking the defaulters to pay extra money, fees, or charges
- not providing adequate and necessary information or facts that the defaulters need to resolve their debt history
- being disrespectful in communication, whether verbal or non-verbal

The downside of engaging in unfair practices is that they will erode whatever reputation the financial institution may have had. This will make it difficult for other borrowers to approach the affected bank for financial credits or loans in the future. This will have a long-lasting effect on the performance of the bank and may spark an exodus of customers. In fact, unfair practices are a double-edged sword that harms both the customers and the collections officers.

Validation of Debts

The FDCPA aims to inspire fair play for both collections officers and their defaulting customers. This is done by granting customers their constitutional rights, which can be construed as their consumer rights. A defaulter can challenge the amount of a debt or call into question the procedures used in calculating the amount of unpaid debt.

In other words, if you owe a bank some money, you may dispute the figure given to you and call for a newer debt estimation or calculation. This is referred to as *debt validation*. The FDCPA enjoins all financial institution to be fair and straightforward with their defaulting customers.

As a collections officer, you are also bound by the law to act appropriately and professionally. When requested, you can use the following strategic approaches to assist your defaulting customers in undertaking debt validation:

- Provide detailed facts and data that may be useful in the final estimation of the customer's debt.
- Offer strategic assistance, such as data confirmation and updating.

- Create a convenient environment in which this sharing of information can take place.
- Pass the right information between the two parties involved in these transactions—the bank you are representing and your defaulting customer.

A great deal of transparency is required from collections officers when customers are doing debt validation. Any attempt to pass on untrue and misleading information may undermine the entire process.

Legal Action

The FDCPA allows debt collectors to sue defaulting customers to repay the money owed. However, this action must be taken in good faith. All the following criteria must be taken care of first.

Consumer Understanding

As indicated in the act, the consumer's/customer's rights must be respected. This means that the consumer must be fully informed about this legal action's procedures. A legal action that takes place in secret violates the rights of the defaulting customer. It is essential for debt collectors or collections officers to work collaboratively with defaulting customers to determine the best way to do this.

Contractual Agreements

Legal actions should be based on prior contractual agreements between financial institutions and their defaulting customers. This means that only signed contracts can be debated upon in a court of law. It would amount to criminality on the part of collections officers to use deceptive documents in processing the legal actions.

Jurisdiction

The legal action must be taken in the jurisdiction at which the defaulting customer signed the contract with the financial institution. It is very important that the location of the defaulter is primarily considered when pursuing legal recourse. When a debt collector institutes a lawsuit far from the location where the contract was signed and agreed upon, such a case may be terminated because it runs contrary to the FDCPA. In general, some experienced collections officers have always preferred a more peaceful approach to recouping debts, because suing a defaulter is expensive and the outcome may be unpredictable.

Deceptive Forms

No doubt there is plenty of paperwork involved in a contract between a bank and a borrowing customer. Collections officers are the representatives of the bank or financial institution to the customer. Customers believe that every form the collections officer presents is valid and authentic. However, there could be instances when unscrupulous collections officers furnish defaulting customers with deceptive forms. This is not only illegal and criminal in nature but also an indication that the collections officer is not professional.

This action of giving customers deceptive forms can occur when collections officers want to defraud defaulting customers. It is the responsibility of every collections officer to make sure that customers are given only the appropriate forms to fill out. Failure to do this may jeopardize their career.

Civil Liabilities

The truth must be told: Collections officers who have committed criminal acts are culpable for those acts. They could be dragged to a court of law for perpetrating a criminal act or be reprimanded and fired by their employers.

The FDCPA was amended (updated) in 2010 to bolster all the main points highlighted in this chapter with a view to protecting consumers' rights. When the law is breached by a collections officer, the culprit or the bank/financial institution that officer represents is liable for civil liabilities. These liabilities include but are not limited to the following:

- The collections officer or the bank can be sued in the appropriate court of law.
- The bank can be ordered to renegotiate, refund, or compensate the defaulting customer for the crimes committed.
- The bank can be punished or cited for undermining the rights of its costumers if unlawful acts were committed.

References

The Fair Debt Collection Practices Act (FDCPA) of 1978 (15 USC 1692 et seq).

CHAPTER 4

Know Your Customers

Why is there little or no effective customer service in the collections industry? The answer isn't hard to figure out: Collection officers do not take appropriate steps to know their customers as they should. Knowing your customer does not mean being too intimate with them; what it does mean is that you should know exactly who you are dealing with. Nowadays, many banks have adopted the "know your customer" mantra, which has become a viable tool for initiating and maintaining secured transactions in those banks or in other financial institutions.

The Genesis of the Know-Your-Customer Policy

The know-your-customer or know-your-client policy (KYC) has been broadly instituted and embraced all over the world as a useful way to combat financial crimes like money-laundering, identity theft, corruption, bribery, and so on. Its components can be adapted for improved customer service. Examples of such components include but are not limited to the following:

- verification of customers' identities
- monitoring of customers' transactions
- risk management by determining a customer's propensity to be regarded as a risky client

- recreation of a client's transactional behavior
- comparison of customers' transactional behaviors to those of peers and contemporaries

The Elements of KYC Policies

KYC policies have, in many countries, been legally enshrined as a part of financial rules and regulations. The Reserve Bank of India urged banks in the country to adopt KYC guidelines after they were introduced in 2002. The United States mandated that, according to the requirements of USA Patriot Act, all US banks should adhere to KYC. Similarly, Canada's FINTRAC updated its statutory regulations in 2016 and implored all financial institutions to take pragmatic steps in instituting KYC procedures in all transactions with their customers.

Since this book is primarily concerned with customer service relevant to KYC, the following explanations will shed more light on what collections officers or their trainers/superiors should do to start paying serious and meaningful attention to their clients.

Identification of Customers' Identities

The first point of contact that a bank or any financial institution has with clients is when they show up to apply for services offered by the bank. It is imperative, at this juncture, that identification documents are duly collected and analyzed so as to practically identify the person one is dealing with. In the United States, a program code-named CIP (customer identification program) has been instituted. The primary objective of CIP is to allow professionals in financial institutions to familiarize themselves with their customers. Identification documents show plenty of useful personal information about customers, including age, gender (sex), demographic, ethnicity or race, contact information (physical address, phone, and email address), and other essential data that banks may use to make strategic decisions about the customer in the future.

It is important to state that different countries adopt different approaches based on local laws and cultures. However, KYC will not be effective if little personal information is obtained from customers. Every step taken in the collections process has something to do with this aspect of the matter. Incidentally, if you had known your customer well, there wouldn't be any hassles involved in locating that individual at collection time.

Monitoring of Customers' Transactions

As permitted by financial laws and regulations, a financial institution can systematically monitor the financial transactions of its customers. This monitoring may be conducted locally at the bank branch where customers do their transactions, or other financial institutions may be involved if the customer has overseas financial dealings. Either way, this operation requires that collections officers play by the law. Unauthorized monitoring of customers' financial transactions is illegal and may subject the collections officer to legal proceedings.

For banks, the major benefits of monitoring clients' financial transactions include but are not limited to the following:

- understanding the financial transaction patterns of the customers so as to decode transactional behaviors
- spotting risky transactions made by clients
- identifying the level of conformity to the banks' rules and regulations
- discovering any attempts to defraud financial institutions or other clients of banks

Determination of Customers' Propensity to Be Regarded as Risky

The transaction patterns of customers can help a financial institution spot risky behavior by a customer. Those who will eventually end up as defaulting debtors may have, earlier on, displayed some risky attitudes toward money. These may include unwillingness to pay off overdrafts, paying late or not paying up credit cards, or failing to fulfill mortgage or car loan repayments. Over time, these negative tendencies should paint a picture of a client's financial habits that may be repeated in the future.

A bank may decide to use the knowledge obtained from this kind of habit to predict future actions of their clients and choose not to grant them loans or other financial instruments they are seeking.

Rereation of a Client's Transactional Behavior

Clients' transactional behavior indicates what customers are likely to spend money on, when they normally buys such things, and how often such purchases are made. By understanding a client's psychology based on the studies conducted on a series of transactions over a long period of time, collections officers could apply such knowledge in relating with the client. Different clients have different transactional behaviors, so it is imperative to customize this approach in relation to a targeted client. Collections officers can do a better job if they already have an inkling of a client's choices and decisions when it comes to money or other financial issues (PRP 2018).

Comparison of Transactional Behaviors

When two or more people are signatories to a loan or other financial instrument secured from a bank or another financial institution, collections officers may lessen their job of debt recovery if they have spent time comparing their customers' transactional behaviors against those of their peers and contemporaries. If Mr. A has a habit of not paying bills regularly, this may be checked against Mrs. B and Mr. C, who are co-signatories to the loans. The collections officers would now have adequate knowledge of the people they are dealing with for the purpose of designing the best method for recovering the money owed.

The purpose of debt recovery is not to create enemies for the bank (PRP 2018). It is simply to allow the bank to continue to serve its customers by providing them the credit and loan facilities they require. If parties involved in a transaction fail to fulfill their part of the promise, it complicates the job of collecting or recovery defaulted loans.

Know Your Local Customer/Client Policies

The table below describes policies, legislation, and rules guiding KYC behavior in the following countries.

Country Name (abbreviated version)	Know-Your-Customer (KYC) Policies and Laws
Afghanistan	A section of the country's customary laws prohibits committing crimes against persons. In this case, customers are expected to identify themselves to businesses.
Angola	Law no. 34/11 was issued on 12 December 2011 and Aviso Nº 21/2012 and Nº 22/2012 for financial institutions
Argentina	A relevant anti-money-laundering law and regulations came into effect in 1996. It requires customers to identify who they are when engaging in a financial transaction.
Australia	The Anti-Money-Laundering and Counter-Terrorism Financing Act 2006 and the Anti-Money-Laundering and Counter-Terrorism Financing Rules Instrument 2007 strengthen KYC laws
Austria	An anti-money-laundering law went into effect in 1994. Current relevant amendments include the following: • Austrian Banking Act and Austrian Insurance Supervision Act, last amended on 15 August 2015 • Austrian Criminal Code (§§165 following StGB), last amended on 14 September 2010 • Austrian Finance Criminal Code (§38a and §39 FinStrG), last amended on 31 August 2015
Bahrain	An anti-money laundering law came into effect in 2001 (amended 2006). The Anti-Money-Laundering and Terrorist Financing Unit (AMLTFU) was established in July 2002 under the direct control of the Ministry of the Interior. The AMLTFU is responsible for receiving, requesting, analysing and disseminating disclosures of financial information to the investigatory and supervisory authorities concerning suspected proceeds of crime and alleged money laundering

Bangladesh	The Money Laundering Prevention Act (MLPA) 2002, is the primary anti-money-laundering law in Bangladesh. Since it was enacted, several amendments have been made, and in 2012 a new MLPA was passed. There is also the Anti-Terrorism Act (ATA), which came into effect in 2009 and was amended in 2012 and 2013.
Belgium	The local law became effective in 1993. However, to incorporate the third anti-money-laundering directive, it has been amended by the law of 18 January 2010.
Bolivia	Bolivia enacted an anti-money-laundering law in 1997. The law is meant to prevent shady transactions between the financial institutions and their customers.
Bosnia and Herzegovina	The new law on the prevention of money laundering and financing of terrorist activities became effective on 1 July 2014.
Brazil	The previous legislations against all illicit financial transactions in Brazil came into effect in 1998 and was updated in 2002 (Law 9.613). The same law was amended in July 2012 as Law 12,683.
Cameroon	An anti-money-laundering law and regulations became effective in 2005 and are only applicable for banks.
Canada	The Financial Transactions Reports Analysis (FINTRAC) 2006, 2016 regulates financial transactions and urges individuals to declare their identities. In addition, Canada enacted the Proceeds of Crime (Money Laundering) and Terrorist Financial Act (PCML TFA) in 2000 and amended it in 2001, 2006, 2008, 2010, 2013, and 2014.
Cayman Islands	An anti-money-laundering law became effective in 1996. However, the Proceeds of Crime Law enacted into legislation in September 2008 repealed the previous law (the Proceeds of Criminal Conduct) in order to bring harmonisation with all other laws that could address money laundering. Additionally, and as a result of the introduction of the Proceeds of Crime Law, the Money Laundering Regulations (2015 revision) and Guidance Notes ("Guidance Notes") on the Prevention and Detection of Money Laundering in the Cayman Islands (Aug 2015 revision) were also amended.

Chile	In 1995, money laundering was incorporated as a crime in the Chilean penal system by law N°19.366. In December 2003, law N°19.913 was promulgated. This law created a specific Financial Analysis Unit, *Unidad de Análisis Financiero*, to prevent and stop money laundering. In December 2009, law N° 20.393 was published. This law established the penal responsibility of legal entities relating to the crimes of money laundering, financing of terrorism, and bribery. In February 2015, law N° 20.818 was promulgated and published. This law established guidelines for public entities about Article 3 Law N°. 19.913.
China	The primary legislation governing AML in China is as follows: • Anti-Money Laundering Law (2006) • Provisions on Anti-Money Laundering through Financial Institutions (2006) • Administrative Measures for Financial Institutions on Report of Large-Sum Transactions and Doubtful Transactions (2006) • Administrative Measures for Financial Institutions on Report of Transactions Suspected of Financing for Terrorist Purposes (2007) • Administrative Measures for Financial Institutions on Identification of Client Identity and Preservation of Client Identity Materials and Transactions Records (2007) • Measures on the Administration of Freezing Assets Related to Terrorist Financing (2014) • Measures for the Supervision and Administration of Anti-Money-Laundering by Financial Institutions (for Trial Implementation) (2014)
Colombia	An anti-money-laundering law came into effect in 1996. Financial institutions had to comply with the Integral System for the Prevention of Asset Laundering (SIPLA) regulation by reporting financial transactions over defined limits.

	In 2008, the Superintendent of Finance of Colombia issued External Circular No. 022 2007 regarding the implementation of the System for Preventing Asset Laundering and Terrorism Financing (SARLAFT) with a risk-based approach. The 2009 regulation incorporates some new reporting standards that must be adhered to when reporting to the regulator. Currently, Circular Basica Juridica 029 de 2014 in its Titulo IV Capitulo IV regulates SARLAFT.
	In 2014, the Superintendent of Corporations of Colombia issued External Circular No. 100-00005 regarding the implementation of SARLAFT and was changed to the External Circular No. 100-00003 in June 2015.
Côte d'Ivoire	An anti-money-laundering law and regulations became effective in 2007 and are only applicable for banks.
Croatia	The Anti-Money-Laundering and Terrorist Financing Act (Official Gazette No. 87/2008), based on the third EU AML directive, became effective on 1 January 2009. It replaced the previous Croatian AML legislation from 1997. It was amended by the Act on Amendments to the Act on Anti-Money-Laundering and Terrorist Financing Act (Official Gazette 25/2012). However, these amendments were of a linguistic nature and did not bring any changes to the AML/TF procedures established by the original AML/TF Act. The new Criminal Code (Official Gazette 125/2011) came into force in January 2013 introducing new definitions of money laundering as a criminal offence (Article 265), terrorist financing, and other related criminal offences (Articles 97 -103).
Cyprus	An anti-money-laundering law was enacted in 1996.
Czechia	An anti-money-laundering law went into effect in 1996 (amended 2004, 2006 and 2008—Act No. 253/2008 Coll., effective as of 1 September 2008) and last amended in October 2015.
Denmark	An anti-money-laundering law was enacted in 1993, with significant amendments in 2006, 2008, 2009, 2010, 2012 and 2013.

Dominican Republic	Anti-Money-Laundering Law in the Dominican Republic (Law No. 72-02 and modifications on Anti-Money-Laundering from Illicit Traffic of Drugs and Controlled Substances and Other Serious Violations) was enacted on 4 June 2002. Subsequently in 2003, the implementation guideline No. 20-03 was issued.
Ecuador	An anti-money-laundering law became effective in 2005: Regulation to Prevent, Detect, and Eradicate Money Laundering and Financing of Crimes (LPML), which should be complied with by entities pertaining to the financial system and insurance sector to report financial transactions above the established thresholds. In 2007, the Superintendence of Banks of Ecuador issued resolutions that govern activities to prevent money laundering, terrorism financing, and other crimes on a risk-oriented approach. In 2010, the LPML added other controlled entities to the list that must adhere when reporting to the Regulator. In July 2014, the Superintendence of Companies, Securities, and Insurance issued standards to prevent money laundering and terrorism financing that are managed through the National Entity for Money Laundering Prevention. In addition to the Regulation to Prevent, Detect and Eradicate Money Laundering and Financing of Crimes, there are currently two set of laws that regulate two groups of companies: 1. Stock exchanges, brokerage houses, and fund managers and trusts 2. Credit unions, foundations and NGOs; retailing of vehicles, crafts, ships, and aircrafts; security transportation services, postal packages services, parallel postal services; travel agencies and tourism companies; real estate intermediaries and construction services, casinos and betting houses,

	slot machines and racetracks; pawnbrokers; pawn shops, jewelry dealers, precious gems; traders of antique and art pieces; and notaries and property registrants.
Egypt	An anti-money-laundering law came into effect in 2002.
Estonia	An anti-money-laundering law was enacted in 2008 (initial legislation was adopted in 1999).
Ethiopia	The first anti-money-laundering laws were gazetted on 16 December 2009. Implementation of a preventive system began in 2012.
Finland	Applicable laws include the 2008 Act on Detecting and Preventing Money Laundering and Terrorist Financing (503/2008), last amended in January 2016 (original 1998, amended 2003); the 2013 Act on Freezing of Assets to Combat Terrorism (325/2013); and the 1889 Criminal Code (39/1889), last amended in 2015 on the part of terrorist financing.
France	Laws have been fully revised with the transposition of the third anti-money-laundering directive dated 30 January 2009 (the fourth directive was in Jun 2015 and will be transposed into French law).
Gabon	An anti-money-laundering law and regulations became effective in 2005 and are only applicable for banks.
Germany	An anti-money-laundering law came into effect in 1993 (amended 2003, 2008, 2011, 2014, 2015).
Gibraltar	An anti-money-laundering law was enacted in 1996 (amended in 2005 and 2007).
Ghana	Laws include the Anti-Money Laundering Act of 2008 (Act 749) and Anti-Money Laundering Regulations 2008 (LI 1925).
Greece	An anti-money-laundering law was enacted in 1995 (main amendments in 2005, 2006, and 2008).

Guernsey	The Criminal Justice (Proceeds of Crime) (Bailiwick of Guernsey) Law was issued in 1999. It is supplemented by the Criminal Justice (Proceeds of Crime) (Financial Services Businesses) (Bailiwick of Guernsey) Regulations 2007 and the Handbook for Financial Services Businesses on Countering Financial Crime and Terrorist Financing 2012.
Honduras	Laws include Anti-Money Laundering Law Decree 45-2002, 05 Mar 2002 (abolished); Special Law on Abandonment of Automotive Vehicles Decree 245-2002, 17 July 2002 (abolished); Law on Anti-Terrorism Financing Decree 241-2010, 18 November 2010 (in force); and Anti-Money Laundering Special Law Decree 144-2014, 30 April 2015 (in force).
Hong Kong	The primary legislation governing anti-money-laundering in Hong Kong is as follows: • Anti-Money Laundering and Counter-Terrorist Financing (Financial Institutions) Ordinance (AMLO)—2012 (amended 2015) • Drug Trafficking (Recovery of Proceeds) Ordinance (DTROP)—1989 (amended 2005) • Organised and Serious Crimes Ordinance (OSCO)—1994 (amended 2012) • United Nations (Anti-Terrorism Measures) Ordinance (UNATMO)—2002 • United Nations Sanctions Ordinance (UNSO)—199
Hungary	The Anti-Money-Laundering Act—Act CXXXVI of 2007 on the Prevention and Combating of Money Laundering and Terrorist Financing came into effect on 14 December 2007 and is still in force.
India	The Prevention of Money Laundering Act 2002 (PMLA) came into force in July 2005. Current amendment to the PMLA in 2012 went into effect 15 February 2013.
Indonesia	An anti-money-laundering law took effect in 2002 (amended through Law of Republic of Indonesia No 8 year 2010).
Iraq	An anti-money-laundering law became effective in 2004.

Ireland	The Criminal Justice (Money Laundering and Terrorist Financing) Act 2010 (CJA 2010) commenced on 15 Jul 2010. It was subsequently amended by the Criminal Justice Act 2013 (CJA 2013).
Isle of Man	The Proceeds of Crime Act became fully effective in 2009, and in 2011 the Anti-Terrorism and Crime (Amendment) Act was introduced. The acts are supplemented by secondary legislation that was last updated by the Money Laundering and Terrorist Financing (Online Gambling) Code 2013, which came into force on 1 May 2013, and the Money Laundering and Terrorist Financing (Amendment) Code 2013, which came into force on 1 July 2013. The types of businesses that are required to comply with the measure to prevent money laundering and terrorist financing, whether or not they accept cash of EUR15,000 or more, are specified in Proceeds of Crime (Businesses in the Regulated Sector) Order 2013, which amends Schedule 4 of the Proceeds of Crime Act 2008. On 1 April 2015, the revised Anti-Money-Laundering and Countering the Financing of Terrorism Code 2015 came into effect. The revision to the legislation included: • changes made to take into account the revised FATF Recommendations adopted in 2012 • changes in relation to simplified CDD concessions • general amendments to improve the layout, flow, and language of the code. In October 2015, the Designated Businesses (Registration and Oversight) Act 2015 came into force. Designated businesses are registered and overseen by the Financial Services Authority for AML/CFT compliance only. They retain their current status with the various bodies (if any) responsible for their wider business competence or other matters, such as the Isle of Man Law Society, the ICAEW, ACCA, CIMA, the Office of Fair Trading, etc. There is additional specific sector guidance for these businesses.

Israel	An anti-money-laundering law came into effect in 2002.
Italy	An anti-money-laundering law came into effect in 1991 (amended in 2004, 2006, 2007, 2009, 2010, 2013, 2014 and also due in 2015).
Jamaica	The Money Laundering Act 1996 was subsequently repealed by the Proceeds of Crime Act 2007, which came into effect in May 2007, the Proceeds of Crime (Money Laundering Prevention) Regulations 2007, and the Proceeds of Crime Regulations 2007.
Japan	Based on the revisions of the Financial Action Task Force (FATF) 40 Recommendations in 2003, Japan enacted the Act on the Prevention of Transfer of Criminal Proceeds 2007. The Act was amended on 28 April 2011 and came into force on 1 April 2013. Several laws implemented for anti-money-laundering measures include the Anti-Drug Special Prevention Law 1992 and Act on the Punishment of Organised Crime 2000. The Act on the Prevention of Transfer of Criminal Proceeds is being updated and will be enacted in October 2016.
Jersey	The Proceeds of Crime (Jersey) Law was issued in 1999. It is supplemented by the Money Laundering (Jersey) Order 2008 and the Jersey Financial Services Commission (JFSC) Handbook for the Prevention and Detection of Money Laundering and the Financing of Terrorism.
Jordan	The Anti-Money-Laundering and Counter-Terrorist Financing Law (AMLCTFL) came into force in 2007. The date the law became effective is different across the industry.
Kazakhstan	An anti-money-laundering law has been in effect since March 2009.
Kenya	The Proceeds of Crime and Anti-Money-Laundering Act 2009 (POCAMLA) was enacted on 11 December 2009 and came into effect on 28 June 2010.
Korea, South	An anti-money-laundering law became effective in 2001 (amended in 2005 with stricter customer due diligence and money-laundering regulations implemented in 2007).

Kuwait	Law #106/2013 came into effect in May 2013, replacing law #35/2002.
Latvia	An anti-money-laundering law became effective in 2008.
Lebanon	Law 318 Fighting Money Laundering became effective in 2001 and was amended twice, first in 2003 to criminalise terrorist financing and then in 2015 to include tax evasion.
Luxembourg	An anti-money-laundering law came into effect in 1993 (amended 2004, 2008, 2010, 2012, 2015). The EU's fourth AML Directive 2015/849/EC was issued on 20 May 2015. It has not been transposed into Luxembourg law yet.
Macedonia	An anti-money laundering law was enacted in 1993 and 2015 to manage KYC policies and requirements.
Malaysia	An anti-money-laundering law came into effect on 15 January 2002.
Malta	The Prevention of Money Laundering Act was enacted in 1994 and was subject to a number of amendments thereafter.
Mauritius	The Financial Intelligence and Anti-Money-Laundering Act 2002 (FIAMLA) and the Prevention of Corruption Act 2002 (POCA) were enacted in 2002. The FIAMLA regulations were introduced in 2003.
Mexico	In 2004, the Financial Intelligence Unit (FIU) was established to prevent and combat money laundering and terrorist financing. There are different laws that apply to the financial sector and the issue dates of each general regulation (or general provision) vary: • 2004—General Regulation for Retirement Fund Management and Investment Companies • 2006—General Regulation for Savings and Popular Credit Institutions • 2009—General Regulation for Commercial Banks and Foreign Exchange Houses • 2010—General Regulation for Brokerage Houses

	• 2011—General Regulation for Microfinance Institutions (SOFOL—Limited Purpose Financial Societies—and SOFOM—Multiple Purpose Financial Societies), General Deposit Warehouses, Financial Leasing Companies, and Financial Factoring Companies • 2012—General Regulation for Foreign Exchange Centres, Money Transmitters, Insurance and Surety Companies, and Credit Unions • 2012—AML/TF law designated to non-financial-sector businesses and professions Most of these general regulations undergo amendments over time.
Nauru	KYC rules and guidelines are enshrined in the country's Financial Intelligence Act 2012.
Netherlands	An anti-money-laundering law came into effect in 1993 (amended 2003). Revised legislation as per July 2008.
New Zealand	The AMLCFTA came into effect on 30 June 2013. Regulations to the act were gazetted on 30 June 2011.
Nicaragua	New Zealand enacted KYC rules, laws, and guidelines in 2009, and they went into effect in 2010.
Nigeria	The Money Laundering and Prohibition Act was enacted in 2004 but has since been repealed by the Money Laundering (Prohibition) Act 2011 (amended in 2012).
Norway	An anti-money-laundering law became effective on 15 April 2009. A new Circular No. 8/2009 was published by the Financial Supervisory Authority of Norway on 23 June 2009.
Oman	The first anti-money-laundering law in Oman, the Law of Money Laundering, was issued through Royal Decree No. 34/2002 and published in the Official Gazette No. 716 dated 1 April 2002. The law was notified by the Central Bank of Oman (CBO) circular BM 936 dated 07 April 2002. Executive regulations for the law were issued in 2004 through Royal Decree No.72/2004. Royal Decree 79/2010 issued on 28 June 2010 promulgated the Law of Combating

	Money Laundering and Terrorism Financing. The executive regulations of the previous law are still effective until the executive regulation under the new law are issued.
Pakistan	The Anti-Money Laundering Act was enacted in March 2010 after its approval by the Parliament of Pakistan. In addition, the local banking regulator, the State Bank of Pakistan (SBP), has issued detailed AML and CFT regulations, together with guidelines on a risk-based approach in 2012, both of which have subsequently been amended, and revised regulations issued in 2015.
Paraguay	Anti-money laundering laws were enacted in 1997 and 2011.
Peru	Anti-money-laundering legislation was included in the Peruvian Criminal Code, article 293 B, by Legislative Decree 736 in 1991. However, in 2002 the following regulations became effective: • The Law 27765, Anti-Money Laundering Criminal Law, replaced the AML regulation on Peruvian Criminal Law. This law was not enforced until April 2012. • Law 27693 that creates the Peruvian Financial Intelligence Unit (AML supervisor; its acronym in Spanish is UIF-Peru). This law has subsequently been modified by Law 28009 and 28306. The Supreme Decree 163-2002-EF, Rules of the UIF-Peru, was modified by Supreme Decree 018-2006-JUS in 2006. In 2008, Peru issued SBS Resolution 838-2008, which established complementary regulation to entities under the scope of the Superintendencia de Banca y Seguros (SBS). Note that in April 2012, Peru enforced Legislative Decree 1106, Law against Money Laundering, Illegal Mining, and Organized Crime.

	On Oct 2014, Peru enforced SBS Resolution 6729-2014, which expands the list of the parties legally bound to report to the UIF-Peru, adding: • individual or legal entities engaged in sale or rental of machinery and equipment • legal entities that distribute, transport, and/or sell chemical inputs that can be used in illegal mining • laboratories and companies that produce and/or sell chemical inputs and have their assets audited. In 2015, Peru enforced SBS Resolution N° 2660-2015 which repeals SBS Resolution 838-2008. This new resolution implements the integral risk management system (under COSO methodology) for enterprises under the supervision of the SBS. Please note that this resolution is applicable to all banking and financial institutions under the scope of the SBS. Note: We are quoting Peru's most relevant anti-money-laundering legislation.
Philippines	Philippine Republic Act (R.A.) No. 9160, otherwise known as the Anti-Money-Laundering Act of 2001 (AMLA), was signed into law on 29 September 2001 and took effect on 17 October 2001. The Implementing Rules and Regulations took effect on 2 April 2002. On 7 March 2003, R.A. No. 9194 (an act amending R.A. No. 9160) was signed into law and took effect on 23 March 2003. The revised Implementing Rules and Regulations took effect on 7 September 2003. R.A. 10365, which amends certain provisions of R.A. 9160, was signed into law on 15 February 2013 and took effect on 19 April 2013.
Poland	The Act on Countering Money Laundering and Terrorist Financing (2000) became effective in 2001.The act was amended to provide for implementation of the Third EU Anti-Money Laundering Directive, which took place on 25 July 2009 and came into effect on 22 October 2009.

Portugal	Law No. 25/2008 came into effect on 10 June 2008 and gave effect to the EU Third Money Laundering Directive. Law no. 52/2003 (anti-terrorism law), which created a new independent and free-standing offence of financing terrorism, was amended in 2007.
Qatar	The Combating Money Laundering and Terrorism Financing Law No (4) of Year 2010 went into effect in 2010. Additionally, the Anti-Money-Laundering and Combating Terrorist Financing Rules 2010 issued by the Qatar Financial Markets Authority also went into effect in 2010. The Anti-Money-Laundering and Combating Terrorist Financing Rules 2010 were issued by the Qatar Financial Centre Regulatory in 2010 and were last amended in 2015. The Anti-Money-Laundering and Combating Terrorist Financing (General Insurance) Rules 2012 were issued by the Qatar Financial Centre Regulatory in 2012 and were last amended in 2015.
Romania	Law No. 656 on prevention and sanctioning of money laundering, as well as establishing measures for the prevention of and fight against financing terrorist acts, was published in 2002 with subsequent amendments. In 2008, the Regulation to the Law 656 was published and issued through the Government Decision No. 594. Law 535 on prevention and sanctioning of terrorism was published in 2004. In 2006, the Decision of the National Office for Prevention and Control of Money Laundering No 496 was published, setting out the local regulatory framework for the prevention and sanctioning of money laundering, as well as for establishing measures for the prevention of and fight against the financing of terrorist acts for the entities not being supervised by specialised authorities. In 2007, the Chamber of Financial Auditors issued Decision No. 91 applying the specific legislation for the prevention and sanctioning of money laundering and financing terrorist acts by the financial auditors.

	In 2012, the Chamber of Fiscal Consultants issued the Decision No. 7 approving the norms for the prevention and sanctioning of money laundering and financing terrorist acts by fiscal consultancy activities
Russia	The Anti-Money-Laundering Law came into effect in 2001.
Saudi Arabia	Saudi Arabia passed the Anti-Money-Laundering Law and Supplementary Guidance under Royal Decree referenced M/39 dated 25/6/1424H (corresponding to 24 August 2003) ratifying the Council of Ministers Decision #167 dated 20/6/1424H (corresponding to 19 August 2003). This law provides a statutory basis for criminalising money laundering and terrorist financing activities.
Singapore	An anti-money-laundering law came into effect in 2007.
Slovakia	An anti-money-laundering law came into effect in 1994. This has been amended several times and was fully replaced in 2008 by the Act no 297/2008 Coll., effective from 1 September 2008 and last amended in 2015:
Slovenia	An anti-money-laundering law became effective in 1994. This has been amended several times and was completely replaced in 2007 with the Prevention of Money Laundering and Terrorist Financing Act which took effect on 21 Jul 2007 and was last amended in 2014.
South Africa	Laws include the Prevention of Organised Crime Act No. 121 of 1998 and the Financial Intelligence Centre Act, 38 of 2001. The Financial Intelligence Centre Amendment Act 2008 (Act No. 11 of 2008) was released in August 2008 and became effective on 1 December 2010. Section 28 and Section 51 of FICA—the cash threshold reporting provisions—came into operation in October 2010.
Switzerland	An anti-money-laundering law came into effect in 1977 (amended at various stages between 1982 and 2016).
Taiwan	Taiwan's anti-money laundering legislation is embodied in the Money Laundering Control Act, 1996 (amended in 2003, 2006, 2007, 2008, and 2009).

Thailand	The Anti-Money-Laundering Act was first enacted in 1999. It was subsequently amended in 2008, 2009, and more recently in 2013 to meet international standards, e.g. setting requirements on conducting CDD, adding predicate offences.
Turkey	The Law on Preventing Money Laundering (Law No: 4208), enacted on 19 November 1996, is the primary anti-money-laundering law in Turkey. The legal framework established by this law has been updated and strengthened by the passing of the Prevention of Laundering the Proceeds of Crime (Law No: 5549) on 18 October 2006 and by subsequent amendments on 1 April 2008, 07 July 2011, 26 September 2011, 11 October 2011, and 18 June 2014. In addition, the government of Turkey enacted on 7 February 2013 and amended on 18 June 2014 the Law on the Prevention of the Financing of Terrorism (Law No: 6415), which further defines terrorist financing offenses and provides new powers to the authorities to take action against suspected terrorist financing. Overarching these laws are the provisions of the Turkish Criminal Code (Law No. 5237, 12 October 2004) and its subsequent amendments (Law No. 5377, 8 July 2005) and the Criminal Procedure Law (Law No. 5271, 12 December 2004), which also contains provisions in relation to the prosecution of financial crime.
Ukraine	The new edition of the anti-money-laundering law was adopted on 14 October 2014 and became effective on 06 February 2015. This replaced the 28 November 2002 Law of Ukraine on Prevention and Counteraction to Legalisation (Laundering) of the Proceeds of Crime or Terrorist Financing.
United Arab Emirates	A general legal obligation on the part of financial institutions in the UK to identify customers was first introduced in 1994. The Money Laundering Regulations came into force in the UK on 15 December 2007. In effect from 2000, the Central Bank of UAE (CBUAE) issued the initial anti-money-laundering regulations under Circular 24/2000.

	In addition, the Dubai Financial Services Authority (DFSA) AML Module became effective from 2004 onwards. In July 2013, the DFSA AML Module was revised to the Anti-Money Laundering, Counter Terrorist Financing and Sanctions Module (the DFSA AML Rules), while the UAE Securities and Commodities Authority (SCA) issued its Anti-Money Laundering and Terrorism Finance Combating Procedures in March 2010.
United Kingdom	The Money Laundering (Amendment) Regulations 2012 extended the scope of the regulations to include all estate agents. It also included a power for professional supervisory bodies to share information with each other and particularised HMRC's criteria that may be used to determine whether an individual is "fit and proper" in connection with money service businesses and trust and company service providers.
United States	The Money Laundering Regulations 2017 controls all KYC rules and requirements in the country. The USA Patriot Act 2001 unified all anti-money-laundering laws after the 9/11 attacks.
Uruguay	Anti-money-laundering laws came into effect in the following years: • 2009: Law No. 18.494 introduced several modifications to Law 17.835 • 2004: Law No. 17.835, with system controls and prevention of money laundering and financing of terrorism • 1998: Law No. 17.016 standards with regard to the misuse of public power (corruption) Previously, Uruguayan AML laws focused on the illicit traffic of narcotic drugs, but they have been gradually extended to other crimes.
Vietnam	Criminal Law issued in 1999 (effective on 1 July 2000). Law No. 37/2009/QH12 amending and supplementing some articles of the Criminal Law issued in 1999) issued

	in 2009 (effective on 1 January 2010). Law on Credit Institutions issued in 2010 (effective on 1 January 2011). Law on anti-money-laundering No. 07/2012/QH13 issued in 2012 (effective on 1 January 2013). Decree 116/2013/ND/CP issued on 4 October 2013. Circular 35/2013/TT-NHNN issued on 31 December 2013.
West Bank and Gaza	An anti-money-laundering law was enacted in 2007.
Zambia	An anti-money-laundering law came into effect in 2001 (Prohibition & Prevention of Money Laundering Act), 2010 (Prohibition & Prevention of Money Laundering [Amendment] Act # 44), 2004 (Bank of Zambia Anti-Money Laundering Directives), and 2010 (the Financial Intelligence Centre Act 2010).

References

PRP. "The Psychology of Collections: Use the Psychology of Collections to Collect Debts and Keep the Customer." *Professional Recovery Personnel, Inc.* (2018). Retrieved from https://www.prorecovery.com/the-psychology-of-collections/.

https://www.pwc.com/gx/en/financial-services/publications/assets/pwc-anti-money-laundering-2016.pdf

CHAPTER 5

The Power of Mutually Beneficial Negotiations

It is an undeniable fact that negotiations take place between collections officers and their customers. However, the question remains: What is the nature or manner of the negotiations between those officers and their customers who have fallen behind in their repayment plans? Are the discussions positive or cantankerous?

Everyone knows that negotiations between collections officers and defaulting customers have always been very difficult and sometimes turn into personal altercations. This is why collections officers are hated and derided by defaulters who can't understand how people can shed their humanity in order to make life tough for others. This book is challenging this kind of practice.

Cantankerous or irritable negotiations come out of an apparent lack of good customer service. Every bank or financial institution's customer should be treated with plenty of respect and consideration. Customers should be seen as the proverbial king whose opinions must count and whose financial troubles must be handled with utmost care.

If you are willing to transform your collections procedures, as a collections officer or as the head of a collections department, the following effective negotiation tactics may be of immense help to you. The first thing you need to realize is that you are not on a battlefront and the person (defaulting customer) you are holding negotiations with is not your eternal enemy. In fact, your professional progress and future depend on how you proactively handle or manage these kinds of negotiations. So pay attention to the effective negotiation skills outlined below (Kelchner 2018).

Analyze the Problem

Instead of spending your time analyzing your customer's attitude and behavior, do not make it personal. Analyze the problem and not the person involved. Taking this significant step will help you give the problem the focus it deserves. In fact, customers will be willing to work with you once they realize that you are genuinely interested in finding suitable solutions to the issue on the ground.

The primary aspect of communication in any field is mutual understanding. If two people engaged in a conversation discover that they are both heading to the same direction (in this case, to finding lasting solutions to the problem of defaulting), they will be more willing to work collaboratively on the issue. Ask questions if you need more data to make your decision—sensible questions that will make it easy for you to analyze the problem, not cowardly questions that will put your customer in a very uncomfortable position. No one gets angry with questions like the following:

- We are interested in helping you out. How far have you gone in securing funds to repay the money you owe?
- How can we can best help you in this situation?
- It looks like you are doing your best to settle with us as soon as possible, but where are you facing hindrances or difficulties?
- We understand it is not easy nowadays because of the economy or the situation in the country; how best can we use our resources to help you pay these debts as quickly as you can?
- How about this process or procedure? Do you think it can help you get over this debt issue as soon as possible?

There is a very popular quote about transparent communication by Dan Gilbert: "There's nothing better than people talking to each other, sharing best practices, and opening up communications." When your customer (who is coming from a position of guilt and trepidation) approaches you, the last thing that individual expects from you is a loud retribution or accusation. Be humane and handle everything with courtesy and mutual understanding, even though the customer is the one who owes your financial institution.

Be Prepared

The truth must be told: Not every collections officer can approach a defaulting customer with the calmness and courtesy described above. This is why there are a lot of problematic circumstances in current practice. The majority, if not all, of collections officers will arrive at the scene of the negotiation with a poker face and a mindset of exasperation and distaste. The best way to overcome these petty attitudes is to make elaborate preparations about what you are going to say, what points are cogent and essential, and how to present these points to your customer. If you go over these preparations for some time, you will probably discover what will work and what will not.

Practice Active Listening

There is a new kind of communication in town, and it doesn't require you to open your mouth every time. This is called active listening. You cannot hold meaningful conversations with anyone if you are not listening intently to what your interlocutor is saying. Active listening is not another term for distracted listening. In distracted listening, you are already tired of what your interlocutor is saying and will engage in passive listening just to pass time. Active listening, on the other hand, involves showing utmost interest in the conversation or negotiation, occasionally getting some important words in. Communication experts have proved that active listening promotes the following:

- mutually beneficial communication between different parties
- an atmosphere of respect and recognition for everyone engaged in the discussion
- the ability of the person with the weaker position (in this case, your defaulting customer) to be upbeat and open up during conversations

To a great extent, people tend to show significant interest in any negotiation or discussion in which they are given equal opportunity to express themselves. As a collections officer, you are not doing yourself any good if you are the only person talking in a negotiation. It will get worse if you are shouting at your defaulting customer instead of engaging in friendly but businesslike negotiations that may lead to something substantial.

Show Emotional Maturity

It doesn't matter what great points you have to discuss with your customer, and it doesn't matter how many times you have rehearsed and prepared your presentation with the hope of finding out what was wrong with the customer as professionally as you could. If you approach negotiations with a lack of emotional maturity, you are going to bungle everything and engage in a huge waste of time. An emotionally mature person avoids the following:

- making snide and despicable remarks during a conversation or negotiation
- bending the truth in order to suit oneself
- treating those who are engaged in the discussion as unimportant
- creating an atmosphere of discord or/and disagreement
- causing other people in this negotiation to feel inferior

With an emotionally mature approach, you and your defaulting customer will see the negotiation not only as a useful way to get rid of debt but also as a great way to build up a better relationship with you and the financial institution you represent.

Engage in Great Verbal Communication

You must be very good at expressing your opinion about the issue at hand and saying it in a way that will keep your customer from feeling vilified and unappreciated. The kind of verbal exchange expected must be cordial and mutually respectful. This does not mean that you should not state, in clear terms, the purpose of the meeting, but you must use your discretion so as to make sure your customer does not feel disgraced or embarrassed. Attributes of a great verbal exchange or communication include the following:

- saying the right things at the right time
- speaking from the standpoint of an understanding and learned person who takes other's feelings into consideration
- delivering messages with utmost care and clarity so that your customer can fully understand your genuine intention to help overcome debt problems
- seeking others' indirect approval through good body gestures and voice modulation

What voice modulation means is that you should be able to control the volume and crescendo of your voice so that you don't come off as shouting or rebuking your customer.

Be Collaborative

It's true that it takes two to tango, even in areas of human endeavour that are not related to dancing. If you are going to hold a meaningful conversation with anyone, there must be some agreement between the two of you, albeit unofficially. This is not asking too much of collections officers; they are not expected to agree on everything the customer requests or suggests. However, collaborating on the main ingredients of the discussion can advance the communication.

For instance, both you and your customer may need to agree to the fact that repayment is late and unacceptable, but the financial institution may be willing to collaborate with the defaulter to pay off those debts. Sometimes, it may be essential to collaborate on the appropriate method to use in securing the unpaid debt. The following are some elements of collaboration that can exist between a collections officer and defaulting customers:

- which repayment methods will be the most viable for customers as they attempt to make good their promises to the lenders
- meeting time, location, and modality required to hold a mutually beneficial negotiation
- primary goal of the meeting/negotiation for the purpose of quickly and smoothly finding solutions to problematic issues
- urgency of the matter (as far as the defaulter is concerned) and the need to be patient (as far as the collections officer is concerned).

Make Good Decisions

In the course of negotiations, several important decisions will have to be made. You will be able to make sensible decisions if you have seriously engaged with your defaulting customer and discovered important facts about why the customer has not made good on promises to pay up. After listening actively and collaborating with your customer, you will be able to put forward helpful suggestions (in the form of decisions) that your customer will act upon to become debt-free.

The best aspect of this approach is that your customer has already gained some trust in your ability to offer helpful advice and decisions. You wouldn't have been able to win this trust if you were abrasive and insulting. This is the main reason it is always result-oriented to engage customers rather than fighting or insulting them. Some of the decisions that may be made during the negotiation include the following:

- mutual acceptance of a new time frame for repayment
- review of communication methods
- change of contact information, if any
- new payment methods, if necessary
- other financial instruments that can be used to offset the existing debts

When a negotiation between a collections officer and a defaulting customer ends badly, it indicates that something was wrong with the decisions made during the negotiation. Striking a balance in whatever meetings or discussions collections officers hold with their clients is key. If we, as collections officers, do not recognize or give room to our clients to express themselves and proactively participate in the negotiations, we are likely going to lose them. They will show no apparent interest in whatever solutions we are proffering.

Solve Problems Effectively

Every effort you make in a negotiation should be designed to find lasting and appropriate solutions to problems posed by defaulting customers. In this circumstance, you will have to display your problem-solving ability. Rather than adding to problems, you should endeavour to solve them in a way that leaves both you and your client better off. The following are seven useful problem-solving techniques:

1. Identify where the problem is and tackle it head-on.
2. Utilize your power of empathy by putting yourself in the position of the defaulting client.
3. Be approachable and display active listening ability.
4. Give others the unique opportunity or benefit of the doubt to express themselves.
5. Create a convenient environment that is good for free and mutually respectful meetings or discussions.
6. Show obvious willingness to help.
7. Be open to new things or learning new things.

You cannot solve anyone's problem if you are not willing to present yourself as an approachable collections officer.

Utilize Interpersonal-Relationship Skills

The status quo in the collections industry is that a collections officer and a defaulting customer aren't friends but sworn enemies. This may not be written in black and white in the financial institutions' contracts, but the attitude of collections officers clearly indicates this. This is the biggest reason why collections departments of many financial institutions struggle to meet their goals.

So what is lacking in the grand scheme of things? Great interpersonal-relationship skills! Collections officers will surely do a better job if they think of their defaulting clients as friends who require some assistance to do away with their debt issues. As a considerate collections officer, there is no more progressive way to accomplish this than by doing the following:

- Reach out a helping hand to your defaulting customer.
- Provide concrete and useful pieces of advice that can actually ameliorate a customer's situation.
- See yourself as a gateway to a better life for your clients and not as a slave driver who is forcing them to cough up money they do not have.
- Share in their pitiable situations and comfort them sensibly when required.

There would be no reason to call for better customer relations strategies in the collections industry if all the above-mentioned interpersonal relationship skills were already being practiced by collections officers. That has not been the case. This is why there is a clarion call for immediate and conscientious change in the approach currently employed by collections officers.

Act Ethically

It is an undeniable fact that all collections departments have ethics and legal codes they observe and work within. However, nothing has changed in the way some collections officers treat their defaulting clients. Some of these officers impudently flout or disrespect ethics and turn their work into a witch hunt. This is the worst approach as far as debt collection is concerned.

To be regarded as law-abiding professionals, collections officers must display a character that is noble and respectful. They must operate within laid-down ethics and legal codes. It is possible that they may be able to achieve unprecedented customer service if they choose to always play the rules set down by their banks or financial institutions.

References

Kelchner, L. "Top Ten Effective Negotiation Skills." *Chron* (2018). Retrieved from https://smallbusiness.chron.com/top-ten-effective-negotiation-skills-31534.html.

CHAPTER 6

The Repayment Arrangement

It is an undeniable fact that your defaulting customer has broken promises. You have the right to collect the amount of money your financial institution is owed. How do you go about doing this? Harshly, without any human considerations?

The intention of this book is to encourage a humane disposition and attitude when it comes to recouping debts from defaulters. The idea of using force or mistreating defaulters has not always yielded the expected result; that is, it hasn't been successful in compelling defaulters to pay up. Since this approach has not been working, why not try a new one—adding genuine customer relationships to the collection process?

Instead of seeing defaulters as the enemy, perceive them as customers who need some help because of financial hardships they are going through. This new perspective can open up a better way of interacting with defaulters and eventually increase your chance of encouraging them to settle the debts they owe your financial institution.

Good customer service often leads to repeat patronage. In the case of debt collection, it encourages your defaulting customers to keep paying the debts owed. This newfound attitude will surely result in a less costly and lengthy collections process than if the old method of harassing uncooperating defaulters has been applied.

What are the proactive approaches that can be utilized in designing a workable repayment arrangement or plan between you and your defaulting customers? The truth is that there is no one-cure-for-all debt policy. Financial institutions design repayment plans they think will be helpful in getting money back from defaulters. The following suggestions are given as general repayment policies that can be applied in all collections procedures used to recoup loans/financial instruments from defaulters.

Any of the repayment arrangements highlighted in this chapter will work if debt collectors approach customers with kindness and humane consideration. In other words, irrespective of the method adopted, if the old coercive and enemy-making mentality is still practiced, collections officers will continue to end up with the same unimpressive outcomes.

Income-Based Repayment Plan

This method of repayment takes into consideration the amount of money defaulters earn as salary or stipend when estimating the percentage of monthly repayment (including interest) and length of repayment (how many years it will take to complete the repayment). There are two distinct ways to do this while applying meaningful customer service: First, defaulters may be advised to pay a certain ratio or percentage of their monthly salaries over a certain period of time determined by the business; the rate can vary depending on market trends and competition offerings. Second, if defaulters have other financial obligations—like monthly rents, utilities, kids' schooling, and other debts—they may be considered for the lowest rate and raise it a little gradually as their other financial obligations are taken care of.

This is preferable to placing a blanket rate of, say, 13 to 15 per cent interest on defaulters who are still struggling to house themselves, educate their children, and have a modest lifestyle. Under those circumstances, defaulters will not only be unable to repay their debts with astronomically high interest rates but also will be unwilling to cooperate with the collections officers compelling them to pay up.

Pay-as-You Earn (PAYE) Repayment Plan

If defaulters cannot hold down a permanent job due to, for example, scarcity of jobs or health reasons, it is advisable that the repayment plan be switched to pay-as-you-earn (PAYE). Defaulters are given a moment of respite when they have no sources of income. The great thing about this approach is that it lifts the onus or burden of proving financial incapacity from the shoulder of the defaulter, and the collections officer working on the case can fully understand the defaulter's situations and work peacefully to resolve the debt issue.

Think of it this way: It doesn't matter how much force or coercion you exert on a defaulter, if the individual doesn't have the money to pay off the debt, nothing is going to happen. Instead of working collaboratively on the matter and fashioning the most convenient terms for both sides, the defaulter will feel violated and the collections officer will feel disrespected. The only action both of you can take to handle this very sensitive situation is to be patient and learn about each other for the purpose of understanding each other better.

One of the merits of the PAYE plan is that it gives defaulters an opportunity to prove they are responsible and willing to continue debt repayment once the issue of unemployment is resolved. There are instances whereby the PAYE plan may be revised to reflect changes in the lives of defaulters as well as new financial policies of the lender or general financial industry best practices.

Extended Repayment Plan

Every defaulter wants to be free of debts, but some may, at a certain point in time, be unable to accomplish this. For instance, even if you are very determined to pay off your debts, it is impossible to do so when you have no resources at your disposal to carry out your wish. In that circumstance, it is expedient for lenders (through their debt collections team or representatives) and defaulters to devise a more proactive method of getting this indebtedness matter settled.

When defaulters are given a chance to defer repayment, they tend to show their appreciation by measuring up to their lenders' expectations when such repayments are resumed at a more opportune time. An extended repayment plan may involve increasing the number of years required to pay back some debts, or it may even lead to a drastic reduction in the monthly rate. Whatever approach is taken, the essence is to see that defaulters have some breath of relief as they work toward fulfilling their promises to their lenders.

Reactivation

Through a reactivation program, customers get the opportunity to open a new account while rebuilding their credit. The customer must pay the total amount due (the arrears, the minimum payment due, and the over-the-limit amount if applicable), which will bring the account to current status. Once the payment has cleared, a new account will be opened for the customer, and the existing balance will be transferred to the new account. The credit line is set at $100 above the existing balance after the payment is applied. As the customer pays down the account, more credit will become available for use.

Credit Counseling Agencies

Credit counseling agencies (CCA) are nationwide (in most countries), non-profit or for-profit organizations that assist people who have over-extended themselves or are having financial problems. The CCA will prepare a proposal to put the customer on a monthly repayment schedule with each creditor. The individual will make payments directly to the CCA each month, and the CCA will then forward payment to the financial institution.

Flex Pay Program

This product offers financial relief to customers who are experiencing temporary hardship through reduced monthly payments and reduced interest, resulting in short-term account rehabilitation. Customers offered this program are those who are willing to pay but are unable to do so due to financial constraints. Flex pay is not for everyone and should only be offered once it is determined that standard programs are not appropriate.

Settlement

A settlement policy is acceptance of less than the full balance owed as payment in full. Typically, the financial institution does not initiate an offer of settlement. However, if an account is determined to be at significant risk of charge-off, a settlement offer may be initiated. Should a customer request a settlement, other programs should be suggested. A settlement can be requested by a customer at any age bucket.

Term Settlement

Term settlement is a liquidation arrangement for those customers who do not have the financial ability to complete the repayment of their account balance through normal terms. The customer has additional sources of cash for a settlement yet cannot complete the settlement payment in one lump sum under the one-time settlement policy. The remainder will be paid in equal monthly payments for up to twelve months at zero annual percentage rate. The forgiven amount is written off immediately, reducing accrued interest and fees and then principal.

Balance Liquidation Program

The purpose of a balance liquidation program (BLP) is to provide customers who are experiencing a long-term hardship with payment relief and an opportunity to liquidate their balance in full. The long-term hardship would be one that has reduced the customer's income and ability to make contractual payments. The intent of this program is to allow the customer to liquidate the balance over a sixty-month term through a reduced annual percentage rate and a fixed monthly minimum payment. BLP candidates are normally four or more payments past due or have indicated a potential for filing for bankruptcy.

Cure Program

The cure program accomplishes one of the primary goals of an account representative: to bring a past due (delinquent) account to a current status. The program is designed to assist delinquent customers who are having difficulty resolving the past-due portion of their payment. The program is usually offered to cardholders who have demonstrated an ability to maintain minimum monthly payments but are unable to catch up.

Ten Merits of a Workable Repayment Plan

As a collections officer, giving your defaulting customer a chance to choose the most convenient method of repaying debts works both ways. For the collections officer, there is assurance that one day the money owed to your financial institution will be fully paid off; in other words, you don't have to worry about having a bad loan written off or cancelled, leaving your financial institution to bear the responsibility for your inability to recoup the loss. For the defaulter, working alongside a considerate collections officer not only makes the process of repaying debts easier but also helps the customer achieve a life that is debt-free.

A workable repayment plan is one that has more than a 90 per cent chance of being successfully applied or implemented. It is the kind of plan that has been designed and amicably agreed upon based on the mutual contributions of the collections officer and the defaulting customer. The following are the known merits or advantages of such a useful repayment plan:

1. It is practically implementable because the content of the repayment plan is suitable for both the collections officer and the concerned defaulter to work together in resolving the debt problem between them.
2. It facilitates the work or function of the collections officer, who doesn't have to contend with a defaulting customer who is not showing enough cooperation or interest in the matter.
3. Defaulting customers can confidently follow the plan, since their contributions were utilized in producing the repayment plan.
4. It leads to better communication and interaction between collections officers and defaulting customers.
5. It reduces the cost of debt collection, since the defaulter is always reachable by the collections officer.
6. It helps collections officers to better understand their defaulting customers' financial habits.

7. The defaulting customer can have confidence in the actions of the collections officer and erase the thought that debt collectors are callous human beings.

8. A well-executed repayment plan can help financial institutions revamp their repayment plans in general.

9. The defaulting customer's credit profile can be improved in the process.

10. The collections officer can eventually improve performance and increase the rate of annual debt recovery.

Six Simple Steps for Designing a Functional Repayment Plan

Having understood the advantages of a workable repayment plan, how can a collections department of any financial institution design one? The following six simple steps should be employed in designing an effective repayment plan that both the collections officer and the defaulting customer can respect and honor:

1. **Make a list of the debts under discussion.** This will help clarify some grey areas that may arise in deciding which repayment plan will work. Different classes or categories of debts have dissimilar characteristics that demand special attention from both parties involved in the negotiation.

2. **Rank the debts.** Put the debts in ranks based on their amounts, complexity, length of repayment, interest rates, and so on. The purpose of doing this is to pay off the cheaper and smaller debts first before going ahead and settling those big ones.

3. **Identify the sources of money to pay off the debts.** This step requires transparency on the part of the defaulter. Opening up to the collections officer about where you think the money to offset the debts will be coming from can make it easier to know which repayment plan to design for those debts.

4. **Focus on one debt at a time.** Defaulters shouldn't make an attempt to offset all their individual debts at the same time. This attitude is not healthy and may complicate the repayment process.

5. **Settling other debts.** Once the initial debt has been totally paid off, the defaulting customer can move on to the next debts.
6. **Building up savings.** A professional collections officer doesn't embarrass a defaulting customer financially. If you force defaulters to use all the money they have to offset a debt, how can they go on to settle other debts? It is the duty of collections officers to devise a way to help defaulting customers build savings while paying off the debts they owe. Defaulters can then have more savings to pay off the remaining debts and improve their credit profile with the lending institution.

All six steps highlighted above can be documented on paper and refined along the way as necessary. The bank, duly represented by its collections officer, will be able to input the financial organization's policies in the repayment plan. This will help resolve a debt problem that may have once appeared unsolvable.

References

Caldwell, M. "How to Set Up a Debt Repayment Plan in 6 Easy Steps." *The Balance* (November 12, 2018). Retrieved from https://www.thebalance.com/how-to-set-up-a-debt-payment-plan-2385869.

Fannie Mae. "Know Your Options: Repayment Plan" (2018). Retrieved from https://www.knowyouroptions.com/avoid-foreclosure/options-to-stay-in-your-home/repayment-plan.

Federal Student Aid. "Choose the Federal Student Loan Repayment Plan That's Best for You" (2018). Retrieved from https://studentaid.ed.gov/sa/repay-loans/understand/plans

CHAPTER 7

Follow the Money, But Use Your Heart

Debt collection shouldn't be a do-or-die process. Some level of empathy and mutual understanding is required to make a success of collecting debts. As a collection officer, you are definitely doing the right thing by following the money. It is your responsibility to do so, but are you carrying out your duties appropriately?

One of the essential qualities of great customer service is appreciating humanity and doing all it takes to give honor to those to whom honor is due. In other words, financial services officials should, as a matter of necessity, bring their human side to debt collections. How can this important attribute be achieved?

Let's consider the positive psychology of kindness. This psychology elaborates on what it takes for officials like debt collectors to embrace a new mindset that perceives debtors as partners in progress. Incidentally, when your debtors share mutual respect and understanding, it indicates that both of you are seeing things from the same perspective. The bottom line is that some amount of money (debts) is owed by your customer, and your customer craves your help and assistance to help pay off these debts. If you can cooperatively work together as partners, you will both end up happy for the engagement.

The positive psychology of kindness requires you, as a collection officer, to exhibit some level of kindness. Do not listen to people who say that overtly kind people are ineffective. The nature of the kindness expected of you is one that will make you listen attentively to your customer's reasons for falling behind on payments and work cooperatively to fashion the best approaches to repayment. You will design a repayment procedure that is convenient, helpful, and reasonable.

Four Elements of the Psychology of Kindness

There are four distinct elements of the psychology of kindness that, when applied, can help collections officers do better customer service in their already very difficult job of debt collection. Are you anxious about shaking things up in your duty as a collections officer and rejecting business as usual? Do the following.

1. Personify Empathy

True empathy requires that you share in debtors' pains and feel genuinely why they have found it difficult to pay off their debts. You are putting yourself in the shoes of your customers and trying to think the way they do. It is very easy for debtors to notice this genuine sympathy in you and then decide to completely open up to you. They will not be shy or afraid to reveal everything that may be affecting their finances.

This high level of trust and transparency will go a long way toward helping you, the collections officer, design the most appropriate repayment plans for such a defaulting customer. In other words, it is a win-win situation. You get what you want, while your defaulters are conveniently paying back the debt they owe.

2. Exhibit Absolute Tolerance

As a debt collector, you need to exhibit absolute tolerance while dealing with a customer. Do not be a bully or someone who stops a customer mid-sentence. If you won't let your customers talk or get a word in edgeways, how will you be able to extract as many details as possible about their financial status and liabilities? It is a sign of intolerance for collections officers to yell at their defaulting customers or even threaten them physically or with words. Take things easy; work peacefully with your customers in order to resolve any lingering disagreement.

You will never gain anyone's trust by being disrespectful and stubborn.

As a collections officer, you stand little chance of success if you cannot, right from the outset, have your customer on your side. You won't do your job successfully if you have only created more acrimony instead of a feeling of mutual understanding and respect.

Most debtors are aggressive. By defaulting, they have assumed a state of desperation and hopelessness. Most people in that condition resort to violence to maintain relevance. So when you approach debtors, switch on your tolerance mode and do all you can to calm down aggressive customers. They will reason with you and possibly agree with your suggestions once they know you are truly working toward helping them resolve their debt issues.

To be honest, this is work. You must constantly practice getting better at calming infuriated or aggressive customers down. No reasonable communication can be initiated and maintained when anger is present. People who are yelling at each other don't have the pleasure of hearing each other out. So be patient. Let your tolerance mode set in as soon as you begin one of those meetings with a defaulting customer.

3. Transform Your Habits

Habits are what we do every time. It is a golden truth that you can't keep doing the same thing and expect a totally different result. That's the definition of craziness, according to Albert Einstein. If you want your customers to take you seriously, change your habits. Transform your approaches.

How about being silent most of the time when you and your customers are discussing matters? In communication, this is referred to as active participation. You will only talk when you want to ask a relevant questions or get in some important facts. Remember, if you are the only person talking most of the time, you will end up killing your customers' confidence. They will be afraid to utter anything that may implicate them in the future. When defaulters aren't talking, how will you be able to obtain the facts you need to make informed and essential decisions?

You cannot transform your habits, as far as debt collection is concerned, in one day or a week. It is a gradual and consistent process. You need to do it consciously in order to become a better person at your job.

4. Share Believable Kindness

It is a waste of time to fake kindness. Your customers will detect such and even find you more dangerous to trust. What you should reveal is believable kindness.

Like debt collectors, police officers are often disliked by the public. It seems almost impossible for anyone to trust a police officer and confide in that person. Surprisingly, however, that perspective is gradually changing in some localities across the globe. Today, we have places in the world where rare cooperation and interdependency exist between the police and the people in those communities. This dramatic change in the way people perceive police officers may have happened due to a transformation in the approaches used by the police in those communities.

Similarly, when you temper justice with mercy, defaulters will recognize this and won't have any problem trusting you. Money issues are a very sensitive matter, whether someone owes you or you are the debtor. A great deal of trust is required to resolve any issues in this regard. It all begins with you, the collection officer, demonstrating believable kindness toward your defaulting customer. It is a natural phenomenon that people receive what they give out. Kindness begets kindness.

Some Applicable Customer Relationship Theories and Principles

In addition to the positive psychology of kindness described above, collections officers may display their human side by applying the following customer relationship theories and principles.

Analysis

The very first step you should take as a collections officer is to identify what exactly is behind the behavior of a debtor. You can accomplish this by analyzing not only the debtor's financial status but also factors that may influence spending habits, behavior, and relationships. The primary purpose of this analysis is to give you, the collections officer, the clearest picture of the person you are dealing with. If you cannot understand a defaulting customer well, you may not be able to proffer the best solutions to the individual's financial problems.

Collaboration

After analyzing the issues surrounding your customer, it is imperative that you collaborate with that customer to resolve all debt issues. Sometimes, handling a collections procedure singlehandedly may complicate the entire process. This is because your customer's ideas and suggestions are not considered and included as you seek a lasting solution to that individual's financial liability. You can organize meetings where you can patiently seek a common ground about how best to help your defaulting customer.

Operation

Equipped with the right amount of information about your defaulting customer and the solutions to help clear your customer's debts, you should carefully execute the agreed-upon debt-reduction plan.

The three principles highlighted above are at the core of great customer service. You cannot help a defaulting customer if you don't analyze financial problems, collaborate on executing solutions, and take appropriate steps to apply solutions. As a human being, you should always consider how your actions and decisions will affect other people. This is the basis of wonderful customer-relationship management.

References

Elias, M. "Can Kindness Be Taught?" George Lucas Foundation: Edutopia Blog (October 29, 2012). Retrieved from http://www.edutopia.org/blog/sel-teaching-kindness-maurice-elias.

O'Grady, P. "The Positive Psychology of Kindness." *Psychology Today* (February 17, 2013). Retrieved from https://www.psychologytoday.com/us/blog/positive-psychology-in-the-classroom/201302/the-positive-psychology-kindness.

Stoklasa, M. "Customer Relationship Management: Theory and Principles" (2011). Retrieved from http://www.opf.slu.cz/aak/2011/04/heczkova.pdf.

CHAPTER 8

The Customer Is Always King

As mentioned in Chapter 1, it is not only in the retail industry that customers are regarded as king. The financial industry is taking a cue from that nowadays. Gone are the days when banks or other financial institutions sat down and expected customers to flock in and use their services. As a matter of fact, the proliferation of banks and other financial centres has caused such uncommon competition that the players in the financial industry must do everything in their power to acquire new customers and retain existing ones.

It is no longer tenable for customers to be treated shabbily; at least, it is no longer good for business. Customers expect to receive respect and consideration from the employees of the banks they patronize before they will continue to use the bank's services and bring other customers along. Therefore, it is wise for collections officers, who are a part of any bank workforce, to embrace a similar philosophy. They should learn to discharge their duties in a respectful way so that their defaulting customers will perceive them as partners in progress rather than a bunch of cantankerous bank officials.

How do you serve a king? This is a very important question. It suggests the best practices that debt collectors should adopt while carrying out their professional duties.

Service Accuracy

As a collections officer, you must reflect a high degree of accuracy in the services you are rendering to your customers who owe your financial institution money. It is not advisable to offer erroneous accounts or documentation during the course of your engagement with the customer. You can never inflate the amount of debt owed or make a serious mistake in exaggerating statements or matters mutually agreed upon. Whatever your customers require, it is your duty to fulfill it in order to help the cause of eliminating their debts. Your customers need your honesty, transparency, and helpfulness to be able to pay off the debts they owe your bank. So don't complicate things by being untruthful or offering half-hearted assistance when they needed your full attention.

Being accurate in service delivery means that you are providing exact accounts or records of their transactions with your bank, doing everything to win the trust of your customer. It is important to remember that a defaulting customer, if properly helped, won't remain a defaulter forever.

Friendliness

The general picture of a collections officer, in the mind of most debtors, is that of a mean, unfriendly, and heartless person who mindlessly pressures defaulters to pay up. As a customer-centric debt collector, you won't want your defaulting customers to think of you that way. That is an uncomfortable impression that will complicate things or make it difficult for your customers to feel at home with you.

Try instead to exude a magnetic aura of friendliness. Be approachable and courteous. Let your customers see you as a friend rather than an enemy. You will surely accomplish little if they cannot relate comfortably to you. You should create an environment of equality and friendliness so that you will be able to direct your customers to the right path.

It is a fact that we all happily relate to someone who makes us feel comfortable and important, irrespective of the situation surrounding the engagement. More than 50 per cent of cases in which collections officers genuinely befriend and support their defaulting customers have reportedly ended in outstanding successes. There is no magic wand in this scenario;

all your customers require is to be treated like human beings, with due respect and consideration. An old adage says that respect begets respect. If you want anyone to listen to you and take your statements seriously, you must display such attitudes first.

Quality of Service

In collection, a great deal of quality of service is needed to do it well. As a debt collector, pay attention to the approaches you are using to do the following:

- elicit information from your customers
- negotiate with them based on mutually acceptable terms
- stick to the terms already agreed upon to encourage your customer to pay up
- outline the different repayment methods and encourage customers to choose the one that is most convenient
- recommend debt recovery procedures to your financial institutions

In each of the processes mentioned above, as a collections officer, you should demonstrate a high level of customer service and professionalism.

Think of it this way: If you have been using force or coercion to gather relevant information from your customers, you are not doing your work appropriately. You'll not only scare your defaulting customers stiff but also lose their trust and confidence in you and the collection procedures you are managing.

Similarly, negotiating with customers in a way that makes them feel like an important part of the solution and not the problem can go a long way to helping you resolve your customers' debt issues. Strike a realistic deal that your customer will be able to honor and fulfill. This entails looking at the matter from both ends of the spectrum. You are considering your customer's capability as well as putting your institution's goals in focus.

Whatever happens, always remember it is purely counterproductive to compel your defaulting customer to pay up by all means. Many debt collectors have presented unimpressive images in the way they are forcing defaulting customers to settle their debts. Debtors have been locked out of their apartments, had their cars forcefully repossessed, or had their personal belongings auctioned off. Those approaches are not recommended for any financial institution that wants to retain its customers, irrespective of their financial impropriety.

Timely Delivery

In every area of human endeavour, what matters most is time. Two collections officers may not have similar working habits: while one is fast, articulate, and time-conscious, the other may be slow, disorganized, and time-wasting. The best practice is that time should be considered a rare and expensive commodity, and collections officers should never be entangled in constant disagreements with their customers—such a working style wastes time.

As a collections officer, if you have a solid solution as to how to solve customers' pending debts, reveal it to them as soon as possible. If you are planning to negotiate or hold a meeting with customers, arrive for it on time. If you are going to use an external agency to recoup the debts owed to your financial institution, do it on time, guarded by mutual understanding.

In the finance industry, time is actually money. Loans and other credits secured at low interest rates when inflation was high may turn into a nightmare when inflation is down at higher interest rates. A defaulting customer may have found it better or more comfortable to pay off debts when the interest rates were comparatively lower.

Emotional Quotient (EQ)

Emotional capability is measured by your emotional quotient (EQ). Debt collection is a truly hard exercise. So, as a collections officer, you must demonstrate an admirable level of emotional capability to be able to do this job successfully. Instead of acting on impulse or raw emotion, you should use your discretion in a lot of ways.

Some customers are naturally difficult to deal with. That doesn't grant you the liberty of putting courtesy aside and acting harshly toward them. Until most collections officers give preference to applying their EQ, it may be impossible to incorporate true customer service into the business of debt collections.

Every human being is an emotional entity. Every decision that people make for any aspect of their lives borders on emotional capability. Dealing with a very rude and uncouth defaulting customer should not push a collections officer into a state of tantrum and revenge. Two wrongs can never make a right.

Process Digitalization

Technology has not only streamlined the business process management (BPM) part of the financial industry but also led to the improvement of communication and interactions between collections officers and their customers. Decades ago, a lot of the documentation in banks and other financial institutions was done on paper. Today, every process in those banks has been digitalized. Some of the great applications of financial technology (FINTECH) in resolving debt issues include the following:

- **Better data management**—Collections officers can smoothly manage their customers' data with the click of a mouse or by swiping their electronic devices. The risk of lost information or data has been summarily eliminated. The advent of FINTECH has given debt collectors the power to stay abreast of information as far as their customers are concerned.
- **Easy communication**—The level of communication between collections officers and their customers has dramatically improved. Unlike the days when telephones were the only way to talk to or update customers about repayment procedures, collections officers nowadays can send an email or a social media reminder. Customers are more comfortable handling such communication than speaking with angry debt collectors on the phone.
- **Improved accountability**—Through applicable FINTECH, it is possible for banks to monitor the activities of their collections officers. This has improved the officers' performances, since they know that their actions can be scrutinized at any time by their superiors.

Customer Satisfaction

All the steps described above are essential for increasing customer satisfaction in collections practices. You may ask why defaulting customers should be given such treatment when in fact they are breaking their promises to their creditors. The answer is that everyone at some point in time has been a debtor, whether for a credit card, mortgage, car insurance, hospital bill, electricity bill, or whatever. If bank officials mistreated customers simply because they owed some money, how would they have been able to retain the number of customers currently on their registers?

It is not an overstatement that customers are indeed kings. They should be treated as such and accorded the dignity and honor they deserve from time to time. In fact, it really makes the job of debt collections easier and effectively doable.

References

Bose, S. K. "Customer Is the King: A Managerial Perspective in Modern Banking Scenario." *Asian Pacific Journal of Management Research and Innovation*, vol. 3, issue 1 (2007).

Drew, S. "The Customer Is King in Financial Services." *Global Banking and Finance Review* (June 27, 2015). Retrieved from https://www.globalbankingandfinance.com/the-customer-is-king-in-financial-services/.

CHAPTER 9

The Ethics and Legality of Debt Collections

Like every other profession in the world, collections officers are expected to be civil in their approach and obey all financial, civic, and criminal laws in their jurisdictions. They can never take the law into their own hands simply because someone owes the financial institution they are working for and they have been selected to recoup the debts.

The Ethics of Debt Collections

The best way to describe the ethics of debt collections is to analyze the code of conduct (ethics) provided by ACA International—the largest group of credit and debt collections industry professionals—to its members globally. The guidelines for professional behavior are as follows:

- **Mode of treatment**—Collections officers should understand the important fact that they are dealing with human beings. They are expected to treat consumers with consideration and respect. They shouldn't be brash and rude.
- **Communication procedure**—As a responsible collections officer, you should communicate with defaulting customers with honesty and integrity.
- **Debt verification**—It is important that collections officers immediately suspend collection activities once they receive a written request from the consumer for further verification of their debts.

- **Accurate information**—In order to determine the accuracy of the information debt collectors have in their possession, it is essential that they carry out a reasonable investigation to verify the debt, identify the person obligated to pay the debt, and verify the accuracy of the information provided.

- **Threats**—A responsible debt collector should never threaten to initiate legal action on debts that are beyond the statute of limitations. Do not harass or coerce people.

- **Absence of frauds**—Do not engage in dishonest, shameful, fraudulent, or deceitful conduct. You should not misrepresent yourself or the bank you are working for. It is honorable to keep all your engagements free of fraud. You are not only representing your bank or the financial institution you are working for; you are also presenting your image or reputation in the transaction. As a member of any international organization for professional debt collectors, you must abide by the rules and ethics laid down by your organization. If you undermine these ethics, you may end up being expelled from the organization.

- **Unharmful interactions**—A debt collector's interactions with defaulting customers should be harmless and mutually respectful. It is inappropriate to hire thugs or gang members to help you harass your customers in order to force them to pay up. You cannot physically assault a debtor, thinking that such a harmful move may compel the individual to act quickly about repaying the debts owed.

- **Confidentiality**—A lot of confidential information or data is at stake before and during the process of debt collection. It is important that debt collectors make sensible efforts to protect the confidentiality, data integrity, and availability of their customers' information. It is unbecoming for collections officers to blackmail defaulting customers for the purpose of making them pay up on time. Also, it is inappropriate to disclose private information. Any attempt to embarrass or harass a debtor in public undermines that individual's human rights. There's no doubt that such an uncouth debt collector can be sued and prosecuted publicly.

The Legality of Debt Collections

There are laws guiding the actions of debt collectors in every country in the world. It is important to set up those laws to protect ordinary people from unprofessional and overreacting debt collectors. In the United States, some of the laws enacted to protect consumers from unethical collections officers include the Consumer Credit Protection Act, Fair Debt Collection Practices Act, Uniform Fraudulent Conveyances Act, and Uniform Fraudulent Transfer Act.

Some information about the possible applications of the Fair Debt Collection Practices Act (FDCPA) has been shared in detail earlier in this book. Generally, the debtor-creditor relationship is defined by these laws so that when one party fails to fulfil its obligation, the laws can provide guiding principles to resolve their ensuing disagreements. The bottom line is that a creditor has both structural and judicial processes to redeem loans and credits that a customer has refused to pay on time. However, the laws demand non-negotiable ethics and good professionalism when recouping unpaid credits and loans.

Take for instance, the US Consumer Credit Protection Action of 1968, which was enacted to protect consumers and their financial records from blatant abuse. This act gives consumers rights that they can cling to when unprofessional collections officers come knocking on their doors. The law grants every consumer the following:

- **Protection**—The law was enacted to protect the consumer in the use of credit in whatever financial transaction they undertake.
- **The right to know the full disclosure of terms, conditions, and charges**—Every customer must have full knowledge of the terms, conditions, and charges involved in their utilization of credit. This is meant to prevent an occasion whereby a customer is unjustly charged for a credit transaction they did not knowingly engage in.
- **Safety from wage garnishments**—The law prevents debt collectors from taking money from debtors' salaries through their employers. This practice is commonly carried out after a court order has been given. However, such deductions may leave

debtors financially incapable of taking care of themselves and their dependents.

These consumer rights combine to protect consumers' financial ability and ensure fairness while engaging in credit transactions. When consumers are given the right to complain, it serves as a check and balance against unprofessional debt collectors.

The good news is that every nation has its own version of the Consumer Credit Protection Act. Generally, the laws are just and equitable when properly administered. While the FDCPA and the Consumer Credit Protection Act are safeguarding the activities of consumers, the Uniform Fraudulent Conveyances Act or its replacement, the Uniform Fraudulent Transfer Act, is meant to protect creditors against fraudulent debtors who want to avoid paying their debts by engaging in fraudulent practices.

As permitted by law, a good collection system should focus on the following:

- **Concrete payment terms**—A creditor should have clearly defined payment terms in its initial contract with the customer. This will avoid confusion and a conflict of interest when the debt issue arises.
- **Timing**—A great collections officer constantly reminds defaulting customers about time. When a loan or credit is set to be repaid, it is the duty of the collections officer to make customers well aware of the defaulting period.
- **Flexible review**—Sometimes it is helpful for the debt collector, the bank, and the defaulting customer to sit down and review the terms of the credit or loan. Doing this can remove any inaccuracies from the debt structures.
- **Pre-arranged sequence**—Once a debtor knows the sequence of repayment provided by the bank or its representative, it would be helpful to follow the guidelines defined within the sequence. In other words, a collections officer cannot escalate debt collection for a debt that is not yet overdue. The sequence of debt collection must be judiciously followed.

- **Consistency**—It cannot be overemphasized that collections officers must be consistent in their approach. Inconsistency may lead to human errors that undermine the debt collection processes.
- **Matching the debtor's behavior**—Sometimes, well-behaved debtors may receive some reprieve granted by the creditors. In this case, both parties are working toward peaceful resolutions of the debt issue.
- **Closure**—There must be a distinctive closure for every debt that has been settled or fully paid. This can be done with a contract or document stating what was owed and how it was successfully paid by the customer.

There are no laws anywhere that permit debt collectors to be rude, harsh, and unprofessional while carrying out their duties. Debt collection should be an exercise where human emotions are cautiously affected and peaceful debt resolution is prioritized by the debt-collecting professionals doing this very hard job.

References

ACA International. "Moving the Industry Forward" (2019). Retrieved from https://www.acainternational.org/default.

Prater, C. "Debt Collectors' Ethics Codes" (2019). Retrieved from https://www.creditcards.com/credit-card-news/help/debt-collector-ethics-code-6000.php.

US Legal. "Debt Collection Law and Definition" (2019). Retrieved from https://definitions.uslegal.com/d/debt-collection/.

CHAPTER 10

Seven Reasons Debt Collectors Must Cooperate with Customers

In the social cycle as well as in financial transactions, it takes two to tango. This indicates that for a debt issue to be successfully or even amicably resolved, collections officers and defaulting customers must be on the same page. They must be willing and ready to commit to finding a lasting solution to the overarching debt problem.

One of the main reasons collections officers or an entire collections department fails is that they consider themselves superior to the debtors. They perceive themselves as having more power than the hopeless defaulters; hence, they ruthlessly pursue debtors and compel them to pay up. This cat-and-mouse approach to doing collections hasn't been working for decades. It only complicates the entire debt-collection processes and causes banks and other financial institutions to suffer a load of bad debts annually.

In the United States, for example, the New York Federal Reserve revealed that for the third quarter of 2018, the consumer debt in the country remained at about $14 trillion. This huge debt profile included mortgages, student loans, credit cards, and auto loans. However, the most unfortunate circumstance is that most of the US consumer debt will end up as bad debt for the creditors. Why? Collections procedures, as they stand today, do not support or encourage smooth recovery of debts owed by defaulting customers.

In 2017, European Union banks struggled with a whopping 910 billion Euros in bad debts arising from toxic loans. If we consider other regions of the world—the Middle East, Africa, Asia, and the Pacific—we can see that the bad debt problem is endemic and spreading like wildfire across the globe

What are the most practical ways to check this dangerous expansion of bad debt? This book has explained, in detail, how collections officers can transform themselves into people who truly understand the gravity of their job. The primary duty of debt collectors is to help the financial agency or institution they represent recoup bad debt and turn that money into active or performing assets.

The rate at which financial institutions fail nowadays is alarming. Their capitalization eroded over a short period of time because they were sitting on a pile of bad debt. This problem became pronounced in 2008 when the global banks suffered a financial tsunami that saw many big and small financial institutions disappear overnight.

Who is to blame for this unending crisis in the financial sector? On most occasions, management tends to bear the brunt of their institutions' underperformance. However, collections officers could be culpable as well for their shoddy approach to debt collections, which may have put their banks in a difficult financial situation.

This book is all about helping debt collectors do their jobs properly and efficiently. The following are seven reasons debt collectors must cooperate with defaulting customers.

1. This Is Not a One-Sided Business

Solving a debt issue is never a one-sided affair. It takes two to tango. In other words, the collections officer and the debtor must collaborate or work together before any significant progress can be recorded.

2. Debtors Can't Be Forced to Be Truthful

As a debt collector, you may be wasting your energy compelling defaulting customers to come up with the truth about their financial status. Think of it this way: You can force a horse to the riverbank, but you can't compel it to drink. If your customers, having been offended by your impudence, chose not to divulge a lot of sensitive information about themselves and their financial status, there is no way you will be able to dig up such private details. You will not know which modalities to apply while searching for applicable solutions to your customers' debt problems.

3. There Is a Need for Flawless Discussions

Even in financial discussions and engagements, two people with two different perspectives can still fashion out procedures required to solve a common problem between them. This can only happen, however, through effective interactions. Several decades ago, debt collectors acted like they were the masters and their customers were subordinates. They shouted at customers and did some unimaginable acts of wickedness. Did these inhumane acts produce tangible outcomes? Not at all. You need to engage your customers in discussions or communication that can produce helpful and practical results.

4. Customers Deserve a Level Playing Field

When collections officers cooperate with customers who are facing huge debt issues, the officers are creating a level playing field between themselves and the debtors. The debt collector is simply saying to the defaulting customer, "I see you as an equal partner in this matter, and we can both work out a plan that is going to be useful for the two of us." Putting your customers in a position where they feel that they are a part of the solution and not always part of the problem will make the job of every collections officer easier.

5. Officers Can Learn from Customers

As a collections officer, being teachable doesn't imply that you have literally become a student to your customer. It simply means that you have transformed your attitude and are receptive to your customer's ideas and suggestions. It doesn't matter how many years you have been studying your customers' behaviors or how much sensitive data you have on them;

you may still be unable to know them deeply. So allow them to bring themselves out to you. They normally do this in their words and actions.

6. Respect Gets Results

Even when you are aware that defaulting customers are not being truthful in the information they have provided to you, you can use your discretion to steer them away from falsehood until the truth is revealed. Do not call your customers liars or other derogatory names. Your professionalism should supersede your emotions when it comes to debt collection. In short, you should always be respectful.

7. Reciprocating Good Behavior Inspires Good Behavior

Some banks offer incentives as a way to inspire good behavior and cooperation on the part of customers. This may come by way of a reduction in interest or a write-off. As a collections officer, make it one of your skills to spot good customers and encourage them to be more open and cooperative. Good and cooperating customers make the job of debt collection easier and more efficient for the collections officer. You should always try to spot and reward great customer behavior.

References

Debt.Org. "Key Figures Behind America's Consumer Debt" (2019). Retrieved from https://www.debt.org/faqs/americans-in-debt/.

Mathiason, N. "Three Weeks That Changed the World." *The Guardian* (December 28, 2008). Retrieved from https://www.theguardian.com/business/2008/dec/28/markets-credit-crunch-banking-2008.

Rogers, J. "EU Banks Crumbling Under 910 Billion Euro Bad Debts as Toxic Loans Threaten Crisis." *Express* (January 31, 2017). Retrieved from https://www.express.co.uk/finance/city/761231/EU-banks-bad-debit-bad-bank-toxic-loans-910bn.

CHAPTER 11

Customer Service and Collections Quality

This book specifically encourages the adoption of great customer service and collections quality in all aspects of debt collection. In every industry, the twenty-first century has brought significant transformations. The good news is that the financial industry has benefited immensely from these transformations, as seen in the introduction of financial technologies (FINTECH) and other improved financial processes. However, the collections procedure of many banks and financial institutions remains the same after all these dramatic improvements in the financial sector. What are the factors responsible for the slow and somewhat unimpressive performance in the collections arm of banks? What are the customer service procedures and collections quality concepts that must be implemented before any significant changes can be seen in collections departments?

Debt collection is a very sensitive business. It is one of those transactional engagements that can make the blood boil and pump up emotions if it is not handled properly. Humans are emotional beings, and their reactions can be influenced by the actions of the others. In other words, if collections officers are respectful and understanding, their defaulting customers will, under normal circumstances, reciprocate with similar positive gestures. Functional and admirable customer service is undoubtedly required in the collections section of all financial institutions so as to add quality to the existing debt-collection process.

The Importance of Collections Quality and Improved Customer Service

Collections quality and excellent customer service should be essential aspects of all collections practices. Unfortunately, these conditions are the most lacking in many financial institutions' debt-collection procedures. In order to add quality to the collections process and improve customer service, it is imperative that debt collectors periodically undertake the quality assurance and compliance processes outlined in this chapter.

Setting Up a Compliance and Quality Assurance Team/Department

In a situation where there isn't a compliance and quality assurance (QA) team or department, putting one in place should be the first priority of professionals appointed to administer quality and train debt collectors in all areas so as to assure consistent quality and compliance in all aspects of their duties. A typical compliance/QA team is usually made up of an in-house lawyer and a compliance director. These two senior officials may work with lower-ranked officers, such as a QA supervisor, QA representatives, and attorneys. The compliance/QA department reminds debt collectors of the laws, standards, and ethics they need to conform with. These include federal and state laws, client-centric requirements, and company policies, guidelines, and rules

In addition to making sure that customers' requirements are well taken care of and monitoring the changes in federal and state laws, the compliance/QA department is expected to carry out the following functions that will ensure that collections officers stay compliant to internal rules and guidelines in their engagement with customers.

Compliance Training

The compliance department is tasked with organizing regular training, meetings, and courses for both new and existing debt collectors. Collections officers are expected to stay abreast of the latest information, laws, policies, and directives. In the United States, new debt collectors are expected to undergo routine compliance training, sign the ACA International

Collector's Pledge, and pass an FDCPA exam before they can be allowed to speak with debtors on the telephone.

Organizational Policies and Procedures

Each financial institution has its own statutory policies, procedures, and guidelines that highlight the approaches debt collectors must take in their day-to-day engagement with customers. The compliance department will reiterate these policies so that collections officers can internalize and stand by them. Debt collectors need to be consistently reminded of the ethical aspect of their profession.

Monitoring and Scoring Collections Calls

It is essential to constantly monitor and score debt collectors' calls to customers in order to make sure they are abiding by organizational policies and ethics and meeting legal and customer requirements. Failure to achieve this qualitative standard may lead to some corrective measures or additional training.

The compliance department should describe, in a working guideline, how and when collections officers' calls will be monitored and scored. The scorecard may even be shared with customers to achieve collections quality and compliance. Each financial institution designs a scorecard, punitive measures, and training modalities.

Managing Routine Operations

The compliance department should be set up as an overbearing management vehicle that oversees the entire collections operation. It should confirm that calls are monitored appropriately, call-calibration meetings are held regularly, and team specifications for new and current clients are clearly defined. It is also the responsibility of the compliance department to prepare and update scripts used in the calls.

This also involves updating the collections manual and tools. The compliance department needs to review disputed accounts and explore new opportunities.

The Three Ms Of Collection Management

Motivating

Monitoring   ## Measuring

The diagram illustrates the three Ms of collection management: monitoring, motivating, and measuring. It has been confirmed time and time again that when the transactional quality and compliance of a collections agent is high, nearly 90 per cent in all the variables, it usually leads to better customer service and higher rates of collection. It is believed that a well-trained collections officer with an enviable transactional quality achieves collection rates between 83 and 85 per cent. That's a pretty high-level performance.

Financial institutions can use their internal and external resources to motivate their collections agents. These may include promotions, salary raises, welfare packages, and so on. To be sure collections agents are performing as expected, it is necessary to measure the quality of their activities. This may be carried out as periodic audits. Measuring their transactional quality and rate of compliance may provide insights into the quality of their customer service.

Call monitoring is a very useful technique to evaluate and improve collector's skills and is, undoubtedly, the foundation to structure productive feedback in individual and group sessions. The primary objectives of call monitoring in a collections operations are:

- Identify opportunities for collectors to improve their communication skills in order to get a firm commitment to pay from customers.
- Ensuring that collectors are following company policies.
- Verifying compliance with laws and regulations.

Secondary objectives may include improving the quality of customer service, identifying training needs, recognizing good performance and improving the relationship between the supervisor and the collectors.

Attitude, Skills, and Knowledge of a Successful Telephone Debt Collector

The diagram below reveals the attitude, skills, and knowledge expected of a successful telephone debt collector. Interestingly, a lot of debt-collecting procedures are conducted via telephone. This makes it mandatory for professional collections officers to exude the qualities highlighted in the diagram.

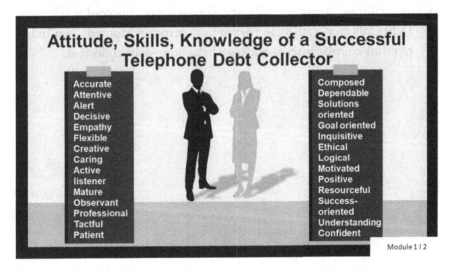

- **Attitude**—Goal-oriented collections officers must demonstrate a qualitative attitude that makes them more efficient in carrying out their duties. Without showing a great attitude toward customers, collections officers may end up making their job the most boring and difficult thing to do on earth.

- **Skills**—Professional and successful debt collectors have skill sets that make them outstanding in their duties. These may include communication, interaction, good judgement, and human relationship skills. They also need to possess technical or practical skill sets required to do their job properly.

- **Knowledge:** Above all, collections officers must have deep knowledge of their profession. They should know the procedures and the right steps to take in helping defaulting customers get out of debt.

References

CBHV. "Quality Assurance" (2018). Retrieved from https://www.cbhv.com/resources/quality-assurance/.

Optio Solutions. "Quality Assurance and Compliance at Debt Collection Agencies" (2018). Retrieved from https://www.optiosolutions.com/quality-assurance-and-compliance-at-debt-collection-agencies/.

Scitron Training. "Attitude, Skills, and Knowledge of a Successful Telephone Debt Collector" (2018). Retrieved from https://scitronweb.com/index.php/full-course-material-packages/telephone-debt-collection.

CONCLUSION

The central theme in all eleven chapters of this book is practical and understandable: debt collections must be done with excellent customer service at heart. Until now, not many collections officers have realized that their jobs are sensitive and emotion-laden. Because they are dealing with human beings whose feelings can get hurt by maltreatment, it is imperative that debt collectors redesign their debt-collection approaches, and that is the main reason this book was written.

It is not enough to incorporate customer service practices in every collections department; the collections officers in those departments must be trained, motivated, monitored, and regularly assessed based on their ability to carry out their duties in good faith.

The elements of great customer service have been highlighted in every section of this book. A question most debt-collection professionals ask is: How do we implement all these great concepts/ideas of customer service in our day-to-day activities? Indeed, implementation is the key. It doesn't matter how long, frequent, and intense debt collectors' training is, they must assimilate these new and improved ideas. Debt collectors must be able to apply what they have learned or studied in the training, workshops, or conferences in their responsibilities.

There are five obvious reasons why the implementation of superb customer service procedures can fail at any collections department:

1. The collections department doesn't have an established structure for onboarding, training, monitoring, and motivating collections officers.

2. Collections officers are not flexible enough to absorb new concepts that would inspire the spirit of customer service, which would be reflected in their practices.
3. There's a leadership vacuum in the collections department, a situation that may hinder smooth application of improved customer service systems.
4. The collections department faces huge budgetary issues, which makes it difficult for the department to allot adequate funding for periodic training and sensitization of in-house collections officers.
5. There is an unwillingness to seek help or assistance from external resources who might be able to contribute new and better ideas for introducing great customer service into routine collections procedures.

Customer-Service-in-Collections Consultancy

Banks and financial institutions have no excuse for not restructuring their collections departments and upgrading them to a level whereby genuine customer service will be the order of the day. If they do not possess the skills and technical know-how to do so, financial institutions can utilize the services of a consultancy firm that mainly focuses on helping banks create an atmosphere of true customer service in their operations.

Printed in the United States
By Bookmasters